T0364245

Expanding the Frontiers of Pastoral Leadership in a Changing Society

Expanding the Frontiers of Pastoral Leadership in a Changing Society

Festschrift for Peter Damian Akpunonu
on the Occasion of His Priestly Golden Jubilee

Edited by Hyacinth E. Ichoku
and Martin Joe U. Ibeh

PETER LANG
EDITION

Bibliographic Information published by the Deutsche Nationalbibliothek
The Deutsche Nationalbibliothek lists this publication in the Deutsche
Nationalbibliografie; detailed bibliographic data is available in the internet
at http://dnb.d-nb.de.

Library of Congress Cataloging-in-Publication Data
Names: Akpunonu, Peter Damian, honouree. | Ichoku, Hyacinth E., editor. |
Ibeh, Martin Joe U., 1959- editor.
Title: Expanding the frontiers of pastoral leadership in a changing society :
festschrift for Peter Damian Akpunonu on the occasion of his priestly golden
jubilee / edited by Hyacinth E. Ichoku and Martin Joe U. Ibeh.
Description: New York : Peter Lang, 2016.
Identifiers: LCCN 2015041433 | ISBN 9783631671238
Subjects: LCSH: Akpunonu, Peter Damian. | Catholic Church–Nigeria–
Clergy. | Christian leadership–Nigeria. | Priests–Training of–Nigeria.
Classification: LCC BX1682.N6 E97 2016 | DDC 282.669–dc23 LC record
available at http://lccn.loc.gov/2015041433

ISBN 978-3-631-67123-8 (Print)
E-ISBN 978-3-653-06437-7 (E-Book)
DOI 10.3726/978-3-653-06437-7

© Peter Lang GmbH
Internationaler Verlag der Wissenschaften
Frankfurt am Main 2016
All rights reserved.
Peter Lang Edition is an Imprint of Peter Lang GmbH.

Peter Lang – Frankfurt am Main · Bern · Bruxelles · New York ·
Oxford · Warszawa · Wien

This publication has been peer reviewed.

www.peterlang.com

Table of Contents

Foreword

I am most pleased to write a foreword for a book celebrating one of our teachers, Very Rev. Peter Damian Akpunonu, popularly called PD, who celebrates the 50th year anniversary of his ordination this year. Very few have had the privilege of celebrating their 50th anniversary in the priesthood. I thank the Almighty God who has given him the health and strength to serve in the Church in a very unique way. These years have been dedicated to the service of the Church in the special area of training of priests both in Nigeria and outside Nigeria. Very Rev. Peter Damian Akpunonu was ordained to the catholic priesthood in 1966 at the young age of 23 by Pope Paul VI. He returned to Nigeria to have pastoral experience and was later in 1967 sent back for further studies in the Pontifical Biblical Institute where he obtained his Licentiate in Biblical Studies in 1970. He moved on to obtain a PhD from the Pontifical Urban University in Rome in 1971 and returned to Nigeria to begin the long apostolate of training candidates to the priesthood. These years of studies prepared him for the future and the long task of training candidates for pastoral ministry in the local and universal Church.

PD's appointment to the staff of Bigard Memorial Seminary in 1971 coincided with a period in which the Church was in dire need of ministers in the Lord's vineyard particularly in South Eastern (SE) Nigeria. The work of the early missionaries who arrived in SE Nigeria in 1885 was blessed with mass conversion of hitherto traditional worshippers to the Christian faith. Their missionary work; however, was interrupted by the Nigerian civil war (1967–1970). At the end of the civil war, the region was a mass of ruin. Public and communal infrastructure as well as churches and private houses were destroyed. The people were psychologically traumatised, homes were broken and most families lost their loved ones. Reconstructing and rebuilding not only physical structures, schools, hospitals and others but also, and more importantly, rehabilitating the returnees posed an enormous task for the state and the Church. To make matters worse, it was during this period that the missionaries were expelled from the country, thus creating a large vacuum in the new missionary land. The indigenous clergy were too few to meet the yearnings of the people. There was a critical need to raise indigenous clergy not only to fill in the gap created by the departure of foreign missionaries, but to expand the supply of pastors to meet the ever increasing spiritual and material needs of the traumatised and impoverished population. The words of the Lord Jesus that "The harvest is plentiful but the labourers are few" were real indeed. The situation required extraordinary intervention.

In response to these expanding missionary requirements beginning from the 1970's, an increasing number of young people were ready to commit themselves to the service of the Church's missionary work. The need for the training of these candidates was most acute. There were few trained priests to take on the task of training seminarians for the huge task at hand. It is in this context that the invaluable contributions of Rev. Fr. PD Akpunonu could be evaluated and appreciated. He returned to the country at a time he was most needed and joined the existing staff of the Bigard Memorial Seminary in 1971. He spared no energy in the fostering of vocations and the training of seminarians. Years after, in 1978, he became not only the Rector of one of the largest seminaries in Africa but one of the most transformative influences in the history of that seminary. He deployed his enormous managerial, administrative and fundraising skills, raising funds from international and local organizations to reconstruct, expand, and modernise Bigard seminary which was for decades the only major seminary in SE Nigeria.

As it is often said, the reward for hard work is more work. On account of his record accomplishments in Bigard, he was requested by the Bishops of West Africa to go over to the Catholic Institute of West Africa (CIWA) in Port Harcourt, Nigeria, to carry out the same transformations. He spared no energy to transform the Institute, in spite of the difficult economic and political circumstances of the period. From there he was invited to the US in 1997, where he deployed his consummate training skills in training the seminarians.

It is not an exaggeration to say that more than 50% of about 4000 priests working today in the 18 dioceses that make up the Calabar, Owerri, and Onitsha ecclesiastical provinces were trained under Fr. PD Akpunonu. His intellectual influence has also been remarkable. For over 30 years, he taught Sacred Scripture and the Biblical languages in Bigard and CIWA and therefore influenced in no small measure the understanding and interpretation of the scripture among generations of priests in the SE and beyond.

The celebration of Fr. Peter Damian's 50th anniversary of ordination to the catholic priesthood is an auspicious occasion to reflect not only on the remarkable achievements and sterling leadership qualities he has provided in the Church but also on our models of priestly formation vis-à-vis the central mission and cost of discipleship in the local Church. I commend the efforts of Frs. Hyacinth Ichoku and Martin Ibeh who took the initiative to collate and document these reflections as part of PD's Golden Jubilee celebration and those who have contributed to this Festschrift. I believe that this is only the beginning of future efforts to document and celebrate not only the notable achievements of Fr. Akpunonu but also many other heroes of faith in our local Church.

I strongly recommend this book to the happy reading of all.

+Valerian M. Okeke
Archbishop of Onitsha &
Metropolitan, Onitsha Ecclesiastical Province
October 3, 2015.

Introduction

Peter Damian Akpunonu (popularly known as PD) is celebrating his golden jubilee as a Catholic priest in January 2016. He was ordained by his Holiness Pope Paul VI (now Blessed Paul V1) in St. Peter's Basilica, Rome, on January 6, 1966, at the age of 23. His call and career as a priest can be described as exceptional, but also his qualities as a person. PD is a charismatic leader, pastor, teacher, mentor, and friend. His scholarship and leadership profiles are intimidating. One can say without fear of contradiction that public opinion is unanimous on his steadfastness, great strength of purpose, and unwavering commitment to the Church.

To mark his golden jubilee, a group of his friends and former students spontaneously and unconventionally put together a number of essays. The choice of the topic and subject matter of the different papers have bearing on the extraordinariness of the personality, character, and achievements of our jubilarian. Celebrating him provides the occasion to do a reflection on priestly training and leadership in the Church, especially in view of the hydra-headed challenges facing it in our contemporary society. One may ask: Has the Church adequate strategies and functional instruments to confront them? Is the formation of future priests and leaders of tomorrow so streamlined and robust enough to tackle these challenges? Which models of the Church are most relevant today? How fulfilling and rewarding is the priestly ministry, especially at an old age?

This Festschrift has by no means provided clear-cut panacea to these issues; it has given some insight and impulse for further discussions. His Grace, Archbishop Valerian Okeke, wrote the foreword. A short profile on PD was compiled by Martin Joe Ibeh. Chike Akunyili, a medical doctor who provided voluntary medical services to Bigard Memorial Seminary when PD was the Rector and has since been a close friend of his, reflected on providing an enabling environment for lay participation in priestly formation. Augustine Oburota, a former Rector of Pope John Paul Seminary Awka, traces the origin of seminary institution and highlighted the need for reforming the seminary formation for more effective pastoral and spiritual leadership. Leadership from biblical and contemporary Church perspectives was taken up by Ignatius Obinwa. He highlighted the parallels in models of leadership across different eras and cultures. Emmanuel Dim describes evangelization as the core mission of Christ's disciples. Patrick Chibuko chronicled PD's career as a formator, rector, and scholar. PD's leadership in CIWA and ambassadorship in the United States of America was elaborated by Uche Matthew Obikezie. Luke Ijezie underscored the strengthening of the faint-hearted as the prophetic mission in Deutero-Isaiah (Isaiah 40–55) to which PD devoted much of his scholarship. Martin Joe Ibeh emphasized the integration of a social mission into the centre of Catholic life in Nigeria, noting that the separation of spiritual and social lives remains a sore point in the development of the country. Finally, Hyacinth Ichoku using statistics and figures made a compelling case for strategic thinking and urgent action to avoid the impending welfare crises facing retiring priests in Nigeria.

We thank the jubilarian for his permission to do this project. We thank in a special way all the authors; they promptly welcomed the invitation to contribute articles in honour of PD. Limiting the number was only for logistic reasons. Our special gratitude goes to those who sponsored the publication. We express our thankfulness to Peter Lang International Academic Publishers that did the printing and delivered on time.

For good reasons, the Church today needs such charismatic figures like PD. As we congratulate him on this important milestone, may God grant him good health and vigour, in order to continue to teach and motivate his students, colleagues, friends, and the people of God at large. This Festschrift in his honour shall not be the last. We believe that the towering academic figure of PD will provide a constellation of future intellectual activities that will address the current challenges of the church in Nigeria, and in particular chart the way for the future reforms in the training and continuing education of priests.

Hyacinth E. Ichoku   Martin Joe U. Ibeh
                       3rd October 2015

Short Profile of Peter Damian Akpunonu, G.M., S.T.D., L.S.S. (Rev. Fr.)

Born on February 22, 1943 to Bernadette and Joseph Akpunonu, the latter of blessed memory, and the first of their nine children, the jubilarian was baptised on February 28, 1943. He was given the name, Peter Damian, because the patronal feast of the saint was then celebrated on February 23. As his father, a teacher and catechist, was teaching in Amaigbo Parish in the then Owerri Diocese, Peter Damian entered St. Peter Claver's Minor Seminary, Okpala, on January 18, 1954 and stayed till June 1959. From July to December 1959, he taught at St. Theresa's Primary School, Ikenanzizi, Obowo.

In January 1960, Peter Damian was admitted to Bigard Memorial Seminary, Enugu. Not quite 17, he studied philosophy at Bigard from 1960 to 1962, and was sent to Rome for theology in October 1962 before he was 20. A Gold Medalist of the Pontifical Urban University, Rome, he was ordained a priest for the archdiocese of Onitsha by His Holiness Pope Paul VI (now Blessed Paul VI) in St. Peter's Basilica, Rome, on January 6, 1966, before he was 23. After priestly ordination, he was recalled to Nigeria for pastoral experience at St. Patrick's Parish, Awka (1966–1967). Later in the year, he was sent back to Rome and enrolled at Pontifical Biblical Institute, Rome, for specialization in Biblical Studies, where he graduated with LSS in 1970. He then proceeded to Jerusalem for specialization and research from 1970–71 and in November 1971 was awarded a doctorate degree in biblical theology by the Pontifical Urban University, Rome.

Returning to Nigeria on December 24, the same year, he began teaching at Bigard Memorial Seminary, Enugu, on January 6, 1972. The courses he taught (1972–1978) were Biblical Exegesis (Old and New Testaments), Biblical Theology (Old and New Testaments), and Biblical Hebrew. From 1972 to 1978, he held many positions at Bigard. Besides holding the positions of House Master and Director of Music, he was Academic Dean of the Faculty of Theology (1974–1977) and Vice-Rector (1977–1978). He then took a sabbatical leave (1978–79) and was appointed Rector thereafter, an office he held for ten years (1979–1989). Even as Rector, he continued lecturing.

His term as Rector witnessed the total transformation of Bigard in all its facets. The much needed and overdue physical structures were erected, with the seminary achieving academic excellence alongside with deepened spirituality. The seminary witnessed talents' explosion as he encouraged all to bring forward and develop God-given talents for the glory of God. The discipline and the proper way of doing things at Bigard were noted and admired by the students, which convinced them that theirs was a seminary with a difference. Liturgical life was impeccable both in planning and execution, with the firm belief that only the best was good enough for God. Cleanliness and orderliness and discipline characterised every aspect of seminary life, which made priests after their ordination proud to say, "We passed through PD." During his tenure in office, there existed admirable cooperation among the Priests' Staff themselves and also with the student body, as the seminarians relaxed and imbibed holistic formation. No wonder his term in office has been called, THE GOLDEN AGE OF BIGARD.

Fr. PD also had a wonderful relationship with European Funding Agencies who supported his projects because of his transparency and accountability. It was because of this working relationship that the International Catholic Mission Society missio (missio-Aachen) made it known not only to the Catholic Bishops Conference of Nigeria (CBCN), but also to the Association of Episcopal Conferences of Anglophone West Africa (AECAWA) that the only condition for missio giving the Catholic Institute of West Africa (CIWA) any future subvention was contingent on Fr. Peter Damian being sent to CIWA as Rector of the Institute.

Drawing from his wealth of experience at Bigard, Fr. PD delivered again at CIWA. He set a record that is structurally and administratively unbreakable. Known to be a stickler for ceremony and tradition, CIWA under PD's regency soon attracted publicity and much curiosity in and around Port Harcourt. The structural transformation of Obehie campus is a part of PD's legacy. Despite his busy schedule, he had time to teach Old Testament Exegesis, especially the prophets.

Nevertheless, the later years at CIWA are not years Fr. PD would look back on with undiluted pleasure. He suffered broken relationships with national and provincial episcopates and friends, and a section of biased and uninformed laity; attitudes to him within his CIWA family became polarised. He came under attack from all sides on issues that bordered mainly on ethnicity and accountability. The accusations were not based on substantiated facts, but rather on shear discrimination, bigotry, inferiority complex, and lack of courage. The once-revered institution PD had to weather a number of storms against him. Written correspondences and auditor reports, however, vindicated him on all scores. He left CIWA for the United States at the end of his second tenure in June, 1997.

Fr. PD had initially planned to spend two years in the United States. It turned out to be sixteen, simply because the University of St. Mary of the Lake, Mundelein, IL, that hired him, would not let him go. He was immediately promoted to the rank of full professor of the University in 1998, and remained professor of Sacred Scriptures of the University until July 2013.

His stay in America offered him the opportunity to reinvent himself and take up new challenges that were very rewarding. Apart from his professorial work, he had time to travel and serve the Universal Church in various capacities. The search for the traces of Jesus, the disciples, and the prophets led him to embark on a number of pilgrimages, especially during his sojourn in US. He accompanied seminarians on annual pilgrimage to Turkey, Greece and Italy under the motto, "In the Footsteps of St. Paul" from 2001 to 2006; and also to the Holy Land in 2007, 2009, and 2011. He led a parish pilgrimage to the Holy Land in June 2013. To date, he gives summer classes all summer on the Bible at the Maternity of BVM Parish, Philadelphia, PA.

PD has not escaped the eye of the Vatican. The Vatican appointed him a member of the Anglican-Roman Catholic International Commission (ARCIC-11) from 1982–1991. As a member, he collaborated in the writing of: "Salvation in the Church" (1987) and "Church as Communion" (1991). As peritus (consultant), he attended two Synods in Rome: (a) "The Special Assembly of Bishops for Africa" (10 April-8 May 1994), on the theme: "The Church in Africa and Her Evangelizing Mission Towards the Year 2000: 'You Shall Be My Witnesses' (Acts 1:8)"; (b) "The Ordinary General Assembly on the Word of God" (5–26 October 2008): the theme was "The Word of God in the Life and the Mission of the Church."

Fr. PD was appointed a member of the International Theological Commission from 2004 to 2012. During this period, he collaborated in the writing of: "The Hope of Salvation for Infants who die without Baptism" (2007), "The Search of Universal Ethics: a New Look at the Natural Law" (2009), "Theology Today: Perspectives, Principles and Criteria" (2012), "God the Trinity and the Unity of Humanity: Christian Monotheism and its Opposition to Violence" (2012), and "Sensus Fidei in the Life of the Church" (2012).

The golden jubilarian is a member of numerous associations, including the Catholic Biblical Association of America, Ecumenical Association of Third World Theologians, Pan African Association of Catholic Exegetes, Catholic Biblical Association of Nigeria, International Association of Mission Studies, West African Journal of Ecclesiastical Studies, and Catholic Theological Association of Nigeria.

Fr. PD is a literary figure of note. As a consultant to the Vatican (1982–1991) and a member of the International Theological Commission (2004–2012), he collaborated in the writing of numerous literal works. He has published numerous articles and spoken at many national and international conferences. He has also directed many retreats and given many spiritual conferences.

His major published books include: (a) *The Vine, Israel and the Church* (2004) – The vine-metaphor taken over in the NT from the OT compares the Kingdom of Heaven to the vine. Jesus, the true vine, bears lasting fruit in his Church. (b) *The Overture of the Book of Consolations* (2004) – It summarises and highlights all the major themes of Deutero-Isaiah. Its predominant theme – consolation – is an inspiration to writers, musicians, and mystics. (c) *In the Footsteps of St. Paul* (2015) – This work – the fruit of years of experience gathered during his pilgrimage with seminarians to Israel, Palestine, Turkey, Greece and Rome – reflects on the historical background and life of St. Paul, his encounter with Jesus of Nazareth and his visionary journeys.

Fr. Peter Damian is an accomplished linguist. He speaks fluently Igbo, English, Italian, French, German, and Latin. Other languages he knows are Greek, Hebrew, Aramaic, Ugaritic, and Akkadian.

On returning finally to Nigeria in 2013, he was immediately appointed professor of Sacred Scriptures at the Blessed Iwene Tansi Seminary, Onitsha. Training seminarians for effective pastoral ministry in the catholic priesthood has been PD's second nature, and he is happy serving the Church in this capacity.

Compiled by Fr. Martin Joe U. Ibeh
May 16, 2015

Patrick C. Chibuko

A Teacher and a Mentor: Reflections on Peter Damian's Days in Bigard Seminary and the Catholic Institute of West Africa (CIWA)

1. Introduction: The Man Peter Damian Akpunonu

According to William Shakespeare, "What is in a name? That which we call a rose by any other name would smell as sweet."[1] Peter Damian (PD) Akpunonu or simply PD, as he is fondly called, fits perfectly well into the best definition and description of a Formator, Rector, and Scholar. Since his years as a seminarian in Bigard Memorial Seminary, Enugu, from 1960–1962, he has always shown signs of rare and admirable qualities. It is of little wonder then that he was sent to Rome for his theological studies that saw to his being ordained at the age of 22, with special indult by Pope Paul V1 in 1966. While in Rome, he applied himself fully to his studies and within a record time he successfully bagged his Licentiate in Sacred Scriptures from the Pontifical Biblical Institute (Biblicum) and later his Doctorate in Sacred Theology from Pontifical Urban University, both in Rome. As a priest, the pastoral work was not abandoned, as he served also as an Associate Pastor at St. Patrick's Catholic Church, Awka, from 1966–1967.

Upon his return to Nigeria, he joined the academic Staff of Bigard Memorial Seminary, Enugu, his *Alma Mater,* where he taught Biblical Hebrew, Biblical Theology, and Biblical Exegesis from 1972–1978. He became the Rector of Bigard in 1979. Within the line-up of Bigard Seminary Rectors, Very Rev. Fr. J. O'Neil, CSSp, was the longest serving Rector for fourteen years, (1951–1965). Fr. PD Akpunonu became the second longest serving Rector for ten years from 1979–1989 and the fourteenth in the row.

---

1   William Shakespeare, Romeo and Juliet...

2. Years in Bigard Memorial Seminary Enugu:

Shannon L. Alder, once said, "If you want to discover the true character of a person, you have only to observe what they are passionate about." The unhidden passion for excellence of PD manifested itself even in the most minute details of seminary formation. He shares fully the thoughts of Karl A. Menninger that, "What the teacher is, is more important than what he teaches." By way of illustration of passion for excellence, his antecedents as a Staff of Bigard included formally impacting positively on the seminarians through his well-researched and skilfully delivered lectures on Hebrew, Biblical Theology, and Biblical Exegesis. After all, according to Donald Norman, "what does a good teacher do? Create tension, yes, but just the right amount".

"There are two kinds of teachers," according to Robert Frost, "the kind that fills you with so much quail shot that you cannot move, and the kind that just gives you a little prod behind and you jump to the skies." PD belongs to the second category. His teaching method favoured those who showed an appreciable degree of love and interest in Hebrew and Biblical studies, especially during oral examinations. As a result, he popularised Biblicum, Rome, where he studied; he prised it as one of the best institutions in the world where biblical courses could best be studied, and many of his students became endeared to him. One observes this great impact on the several priests and bishops who graduated with great honours from Biblicum and Urban University.

William Arthur Ward made this distinction: "The mediocre teacher tells. The good teacher explains. The superior teacher demonstrates. The great teacher inspires." Akpunonu best represents a biblical guru who aptly blends very high scholarship in the classroom with highly edifying homilies in liturgical celebrations. One finds his deeply rooted biblical spirituality evident in his insightful counsels. At the altar and pulpit he does what he knows best to the admiration and edification of overwhelming docile seminarians. To date, his impact on the seminarians in matters of liturgical celebrations remains evergreen.

His strong belief in the liturgy of the Church led him to the firm conviction that every liturgical celebration demands by its very nature elaborate preparation and to take nothing for granted. The liturgy demands essentially a homily, which means a commentary on the Word in relation to the particular mystery being celebrated. As a biblical exegete with particular emphasis on the Old Testament, he brought his expertise on Deutero-Isaiah to bear on the quality of his liturgical celebrations in general and on the homily in particular.

In him is found a perfect fulfilment of what a homily ought to be, namely, a commentary on the word. In the liturgical celebrations, biblical texts are approached first with their brief and illustrative background, uncomplicated exegesis leading ultimately to a functional biblical message enriched with challenges for the edification of the Church in her members. It became clear for the seminarians to see a clear nexus between scholarship and praxis.

He paid particular attention to the Choir. As director of the Seminary Choir, the members of Bigard Choir still recall the green memories of their seminary days, especially the positive impact liturgical music made on them. With the teaching instinct in him, he made singing admirable for all the seminarians. The members of the choir benefitted a great deal by his simplifying of even the complicated classical music of Beethoven, Mozart, Bach, Handel, etc. These became familiar tunes although one can never be too familiar with classical tunes. Such compositions certainly improved a great deal the level of intelligence and the degree of appreciation of values of the choristers.

2.1 Major Achievements in Bigard Seminary, Enugu

Official history will bear witness to the remarkable achievements PD made in Bigard. First Papal Visit to Nigeria in 1982; initially Bigard Memorial Seminary was not on the list of the places to be visited by the Pope, but PD succeeded in making it possible and was outstanding in both planning and hosting the Papal Visit of Pope St. John Paul. This unprecedented visit transformed the image of the Seminary into a mini St. Peter's Square even for the few days before and after. Within the overall plan of the First Papal Pastoral Visit to Nigeria, the Holy Father was to meet and address the Nigerian Priests in Enugu. Thanks as well to the generosity of the then Executive Governor of Anambra State, Chief Jim Ifeanyichukwu Nwobodo, who co-hosted the papal visit in an unprecedented manner.

PD's regime in Bigard attracted special and generous benefactors and benefactress to the Seminary, especially the double visit of Governor Nwobodo. The evidence of which are still living with us today in the tarring of the Bigard avenues and the erection of St. James ultra-modern library. During his regime, Governor Bob Akonobi identified with Bigard through the personality of PD and that earned the Seminary a very gigantic electric generator that catered conveniently to the dire energy needs of the Seminary. The Deacons' hostel called Vatican Hostel, the two modern Priests' Staff Quarters, the huge capacity Auditorium, and a Class Room of three floors as his last act in Bigard stand today to testify to the colossus of a man of great achievements for God and for humanity.

Seminarians enjoyed personal scholarships from overseas benefactors and benefactresses, although with the strict regulation of anonymity to forestall some common abuses on the part of the seminarians until they get ordained as priests. He not only promoted academic excellence, he regularly encouraged and contributed to the Seminary Journal called *Bigard Theological Studies*. Indeed, during his tenure as Rector, the Seminary enjoyed tremendous development in intellectual, spiritual, pastoral, human, and social perspectives. He believed in the use of social media for the integral development and education of the contemporary seminarians. The fortnightly film shows that PD introduced exposed seminarians to the right perspectives of modern society they are to serve later as priests. Consequently, other useful social media began to be introduced into the seminary lifestyle.

2.2 Some Testimonies about PD from the Bigard Seminary

It was Aristotle who said, "Those who educate children well are more to be honoured than they who produce them; for these only gave them life, those, the art of living well." And this was corroborated by Alexander the Great when he said, "I am indebted to my father for living, but to my teacher for living well". *His teacher was the legendary philosopher* Aristotle. PD perfectly fits into this description. The teacher instinct in him earned him the following accolades of inspiring testimonies.

It was his first sabbatical leave in Bigard after six years of teaching. The following were said of him by the members of Bigard's junior staff: "Your six years stay in Bigard Seminary have been both productive and progressive and there is no doubt that both as an ordinary member of the academic staff, as a Dean and presently as a Vice Rector, you have had a wealth of experience and insight into what staying in such a place as Bigard means and entails. We hope your experiences here for these six years will only make you all the more resolute to put in more years in the future and the sabbatical leave will go a long way in bringing you back to us wholly refreshed and drooping with fresh blood for added work in this difficult, but all the same, sweet section of the Lord's vineyard. You leave us now as a Vice Rector, who knows if you will not come back to become a full time Rector? If it pleases God, it will please us too."[2]

Referring to PD as a teacher within the liturgical celebrations, the staff observed thus: "Father, your occasional sermons to us here proves you a competent Scripture Master, and one who speaks out of conviction. Your explanation of Scripture texts and the examples which you employ to do this make the understanding of what you are after clear and simple and thus we hardly forget the lesson of the day and the scriptural texts in question. All this is to your credit."[3]

On human relationship, "your decisions in matters of importance manifest your maturity, although your huge bearing and look, like a fierce lion ready for action at any time, can deceive a fellow who is not near you often and give him a mistaken impression, whereas you are full of charity, sincerity, joviality, energy, straightforwardness and affability – in fact a perfect gentleman."[4]

On the same occasion of his send-off, the students underscored PD's shining examples of flexibility, sacrifice, sensitivity, and understanding: "Father, you were due for a Sabbatical leave last academic session but since you were the sole Scripture Professor then, you offered to put in another year pending on the time we will get another professor of Sacred Scripture. We appreciate this sacrifice of yours."[5]

---

2 (Previous reference is incomplete) A Send-off Address Presented By the Bigard Junior Staff to Very Rev. Fr. P. D. Akpunonu On Sabbatical Leave, May 29, 1978.
3 A Send-off Address by the Bigard Junior Staff, 1978.
4 A Send-off Address by the Bigard Junior Staff, 1978.
5 A Send-off Address Presented to Rev. Fr. P. D. Akpunonu by the Students of Bigard Memorial Seminary, Enugu on the Occasion of his Sabbatical Leave, May 29, 1978.

Appreciating the quality teacher they had in PD, the students testified thus: "When you arrived here in 1972 to join the Bigard staff you did not waste time to reveal to us the academic packages you brought from Rome after defending your doctoral thesis in Sacred Theology (STD) and Licentiate in Sacred Scripture (LSS). Your first class was interesting and so exciting that the students after the class felt that the academic Messiah had come. You opened the infinite treasures of the Bible for many students and your explanation sounded a big relief to those who were perplexed about the Scriptures."[6]

During his recent visit to Bigard, the staff and students could not conceal their lurking sentiments when they said: "Playing host to a visitor could be interesting. But playing host to a grand Dad is not only interesting but goes with nostalgic feelings and could have some rituals and strings of religiosity attached. Such were the feelings sparked off by the reception organized by the Bigard family, in honour of her one time Rector, Very Rev. Fr. Prof. Peter-Damian Akpunonu; a Catholic priest of Onitsha Archdiocese."[7]

On his own part, Rev. Fr. Dr. Theophilus Ukoro Igwe, the Rector at this reception, bared his mind thus on Akpunonu when he said: "We are grateful to God Almighty for His innumerable gifts to us and especially for the gift of our own dear Rector, formator, and teacher, Rev. Fr. Prof. Peter Damian Akpunonu, whose profound presence we enjoy here tonight."[8] Ukoro Igwe went further to say that the guest that, "we are celebrating was not just for the fact of his committed service in the Lord's vineyard, but also because; through him Bigard has attained great heights."[9]

Ukoro Igwe carefully unravelled the intimidating profiles and sterling qualities of Fr. Prof Peter Damian, hidden underneath his simplicity and humility. Ukoro went further to highlight that Fr. Prof. Akpunonu, "was a seminarian of Bigard from 1960 to 1962, and was ordained at the age of 23, with special indult by Pope Paul VI in the year 1966. He was the Rector of Bigard from 1979–1989. All of us gathered here tonight can rightly claim to be your students directly or indirectly. This is because

---

6   A Send-off Address by the Students, 1978.
7   Welcome Address, 2nd March, 2014.
8   Welcome Address, 2nd March, 2014.
9   Welcome Address, 2nd March, 2014.

you taught some of us directly, who are now teaching others."According to Ukoro, Fr. Prof. Akpunonu, after his function as a Rector at the Catholic Institute of West Africa (CIWA) between 1989 and 1997, proceeded to teach Biblical Exegesis at the University of St. Mary of Lake – Mundelein Seminary, in the Archdiocese of Chicago.

In that same visit, Prof. PD Akpunonu left with the seminarians some food for thought that would guide them safely for life as exemplary priests. He advised them that Seminary was a place where things were well done. They should, therefore, let external decorum be only an index of the authentic and holistic formation that they were receiving. There should be no half measures as far as integral formation and contemporary priesthood were concerned because only the best was good enough for Bigard Seminary. He pointed out to the seminarians that the best God could do for any human being was to make one a priest. In his own words, he said, "Tell me what more God could have done for you than making you a priest. That is why you should take your formation very seriously."

He went further to underscore some key points in the seminary formation thus: "You should be able to incarnate Jesus Christ in time and space. And therefore, my dear seminarians please, do not allow worldly things to distract you." To illustrate this point further, he observed, "Anything that you will not be proud of on your death-bed does not belong to you. Anything, for which you could be embarrassed if anybody found out, does not belong to you." He disclosed that "seminarians should remain focussed because, the only joy in being a priest was to conscientiously every day, try to be a very good and a very holy priest." "When you begin to compromise, when you begin to cut corners that is when there is a problem," he concluded.

During that same visit to Bigard on March 2–3, 2014, the beautiful blend of biblical expertise and liturgical celebration came to the fore. According to the Seminary Journalist, "Rev. Fr. Prof. Peter-Damian Akpunonu presided over the Mass of Monday March 3, 2014. In his homily, his being a Professor in biblical exegesis was made manifest again as he soaked the minds of all present into the readings of the day, downloading, packaging and applying the readings to the concrete circumstance of the worshipping assembly's daily life."[10] According to him; "One of the major reasons why we do not fulfil our ministerial duties, which we are called to is that all of us have some sort of attachment."[11] The climax of his visit was the coronation and designation as the Formator of formators and Rector of rectors, the '*Nnazuruoha 1* of Bigard' (the father who trained all) according to the Bigard family.[12]

3. PD Akpunonu and the Catholic Institute of West Africa (CIWA) Port Harcourt

With the end of the tenure of the Second Rector of CIWA, late Msgr. C. S. Mbah, who succeeded the premier Rector late Most Rev. S. N. Ezeanya, there arose a serious need for a third one. It was at this point that missio Aachen intervened with regard to the choice of a new Rector of CIWA. To put it more graphically, CIWA had been taxing on the runway since its inception and missio Aachen said it had spotted the right individual to lift CIWA up from the runway. It asked that the then Rector of Bigard Memorial Seminary, Enugu, Rev. Fr. Dr. Peter Damian Akpunonu be transferred to CIWA. The Bishops of AECAWA and CBCN in particular were in agreement and assured Fr. PD Akpunonu maximum cooperation. Relying on this trust and good-will, the new Rector assumed office on July 1, 1989, hoping to give CIWA a new lease of life.

It will be of interest to recall that his first physical contact with CIWA Port Harcourt was the very day; the Bigard Seminarians in great numbers (with fleet of vehicles) in a convoy accompanied him from Bigard Enugu to CIWA. Like St. Paul, he transferred his dynamic zeal and avowed uncommon credentials in administration to CIWA. Coming to CIWA was for him like the biblical call soliciting Paul to come over to Macedonia to help out. With his arrival in CIWA, the status quo changed remarkably in all scores.

---

10 Bigard Memorial Seminary, Enugu, Journalist, 3rd March, 2014.
11 Bigard Memorial Seminary, Enugu, Journalist, 3rd March, 2014.
12 Welcome Address on the Happy Occasion of Bigard Family Receiving and Welcoming One of Her Emeritus Rectors, Rev. Fr. Prof. Peter-Damian Akpunonu, 2ndMarch, 2014.

3.1 PD Akpunonu and the CIWA Governing Council 1989–1997

During his years in CIWA, every aspect of the Institute not only received adequate attention but assumed a higher level of development. Governing Council meetings were regular. They were preceded by a series of feeder meetings in an effort to carry everyone along. The Faculty Board, All Staff Meeting, and Senate would meet many weeks before the Governing Council. This made it possible for the Council to have first-hand information and experiences of what CIWA was doing, and her challenges and achievements. Weeks preceding Council meetings were distinguished by beehive activities in every sector of the Institute, especially preparing documents and files which would be distributed to the members immediately on arrival so that they could read them before the general assembly. The effects of such preparations were usually enormous and point to the dexterity in administration of PD Akpunonu.

The liturgical celebrations of that week were usually elaborate and begun with the Exposition of the Blessed Sacrament, Eucharistic Celebration often combined with Lauds and the liturgical functions distributed across the mixed Bishop members of the Council from Nigeria, Ghana, Sierra Leone, Liberia, the Gambia, and other experts from different walks of life from Nigerian and SECAM representatives.

An outstanding achievement of PD Akpunonu with the Council was in 1995 with the launch of the Catholic University of West Africa (CUWA). What CIWA is still battling today to do in order to get the Nigerian University Commission (NUC) grant the request for autonomy would have been a foregone conclusion if not for the Nigerian factor. As an insider in the negotiation for the University status for CIWA, our consultations with representatives of the Nigerian University Commission (NUC) ended up positively that CIWA had enough land, required infrastructure to take off and the amount of money required would not be a problem since CIWA did not have to show the physical cash, but could request one of the Bishops of AECAWA to stand in as surety. CUWA was eventually launched in 1995. That launch is still seen as the threshold of some of the Residential Blocks where the Academic Staff members live at Obehie, saying, "Welcome to CUWA," to this day.

3.2 PD Akpunonu and the Catholic Bishops Conference of Nigeria 1989–1997

In his years in administration, the CBCN frequently visited CIWA on different occasions for one function or the other; such as, the opening of the academic year, theology week celebrations and since the CBCN had its representative in the Council, the Chairman had more opportunities to visit and interact with both staff and students.

3.3 PD Akpunonu and Port Harcourt Diocese 1989–1997

With Port Harcourt Diocese, PD worked in synergy with Bishops Edward Fitzgibbon and Alexius Makozi as well as the clergy, religious, and the laity of the diocese largely on an official basis. The Rector had a rare advantage, as more than three quarters of the priests in the diocese of Port Harcourt passed through him in Bigard either as a lecturer or Rector or both. He knew practically all the priests by name, even their popular names, and interacted with everyone. Among the laity, such personalities as the Allagoa family: the Mingi, Victor Allagoa, the Barrister, and others were his close allies and were very handy. Many of the prominent contractors who worked at Obehie were drawn from PH; such as, Mr. Precious. These were tested and trusted collaborators.

3.4 Land and Ethnicity: Perennial Problem of CIWA

The truth remains that when PD Akpunonu arrived at CIWA in 1989 the underlying problems of the Institute were already there, especially Land and Ethnicity. With regard to land acquisition for CIWA, it was unfortunate that Port Harcourt Diocese could not come up with the land it had promised CBCN and AECAWA over and over again. When the Rector had secured funds for seven buildings and the money was not used for two years, because land was not available, and as the donors became more restless, anxiety grew in AECAWA. Consequently, AECAWA told CBCN to find a solution to the land issue before the next meeting of the Governing Council. Hence CBCN asked Council to get a site "in or around PH."

When all efforts to get property in Port Harcourt failed, an alternative site was found in Obehie. Though in Aba Diocese, this site was nevertheless very close to Port Harcourt. Council visited and approved of the site and asked the Rector to move into the new site with great speed to recoup for the lost time.

This decision of Council did not go down well with many members of the CBCN – the only reason being that the location was in Igboland. Since no one wanted to put the blame on Council, it was believed to be less risky to lay the blame squarely on the Rector, making him the scapegoat. So out went the statement: "The Rector of CIWA singlehandedly moved CIWA from Port Harcourt to Obehie."

Such a statement caused initial surprise, which was followed by an uproar and was physically demonstrated by the protest of priests and some members of the laity of the Port Harcourt Diocese. Furthermore, people began to wonder what type of man could dare to do such a thing. The reply was that he was used to doing outrageous things as running CIWA singlehandedly, without reference to the Statutes; that he had no respect for the Bishop of PH and of Council Chairman; that he did not call meetings; that he appointed officials to positions even when the Statutes clearly stipulated that such positions were elective; that accounts were neither audited nor submitted to anyone; and that because he relied on his ability to raise funds overseas, he would leave the country at will without permission and return at will too.

3.5 A Providential Meeting in Rome

The Rector, by chance, travelled to Rome, as he had a meeting with the then Secretary General of *Opus Sancti Petri Apostoli*. While in his office, he was told that the Cardinal Prefect of the Evangelization of the Peoples wanted to see him. On arriving at his office, he was met with two other very high officials of the congregation and a secretary.

Lo and behold, he was before a tribunal, without warning and without preparation. The above six charges and a few minor others were put before him and he was given ample opportunity to defend himself. He explained the cases one after the other and promised to submit all the relevant documents later to back up his case. With the submission of the documents, he was completely exonerated, and those who sent the allegations did not create the best image for themselves.

Despite that, the Rector was able to erect 22 buildings in 30 months at Obehie Campus and would have handed over to AECAWA a full-fledged university, Catholic University of West Africa (CUWA) in another two years, were it not for the Nigerian factor.

3.6 The Nigerian Factor

A delegation of the CBCN visited the major funding agencies; such as, *Opus Sancti Petri, Rome, missio Aachen, and missio Munich* and alleged that all the troubles at CIWA were the Rector's. They alleged that the Rector had usurped all authority at CIWA – academics, administration, and had of late taken over projects; that he did not give the Bishops of Nigeria the opportunity to play their part but rather gave the funding agencies the impression that the CBCN was not interested in the physical development of CIWA. The Rector should be instructed to be "hands-off" on all projects at CIWA and this would see the quick development at CIWA.

Incidentally, it happened that shortly before the trip of the CBCN delegation, the Rector, had made the most successful trip of his carrier and had raised almost a million US dollars which would have completed and equipped all the buildings on the master plan. The Rector was instructed by the CIWA Governing Council to have nothing to do with projects any more and for the last two years in office, no new physical development took place. The CBCN has yet to fulfil the promise purported to be made in her name by the delegation.

3.7 Another Providential Meeting in Rome

Even though the CIWA was an ecclesiastical tertiary institution, it was not chartered by the Congregation for Catholic Education. Before the First African Synod in 1994, the process to get CIWA chartered was initiated, and completed during the Synod. At that Synod, the President of AECAWA, the Chancellor, and the Rector of CIWA had a meeting with the Prefect, the Secretary, and the top officials of the Congregation for Catholic Education, as well as, with the Prefect of the Congregation for the Evangelization of the Peoples. At the end of the Synod, the Congregation for Catholic Education approved CIWA Statutes and Curriculum of Studies, appointed the Chancellor, the Rector and the Academic Dean, and chartered CIWA for the

STL. The Prefect of the Congregation for the Evangelization of the Peoples agreed to release the funds of CIWA which had been withheld.

It was there that the Prefect added, that he had reports that the Rector had built a mansion in his village with the money from CIWA. Meanwhile he, the Prefect, had conducted his investigations and found the reports false, adding that if there were any foundation to the reports, he would relieve himself of his office.

Again, in 1996, an allegation was brought to the Council that the Rector's administration was bedevilled with ethnicity. The Rector sent a memo to all of the AECAWA in which he listed all the senior staff at CIWA upon assuming office and a list of senior staff at the present moment. It turned out that before his first year in office, all the senior administrative staff were Igbos, except the Bursar who was from Ghana, and who left soon after his arrival. In his own year in question, all the senior administrative staff were non-Igbos except the Rector and the Bursar. The reason why the Bursar was an Igbo was that no diocese was willing to give CIWA a Bursar, until Onitsha Archdiocese out of compassion gave one of her priests.

The Council then decided to send an investigation panel to CIWA. Most interestingly, the Panel had all the time to plan the work, but did not inform the Rector of the date of the visit. The Rector was attending a meeting in Argentina when the Panel arrived at CIWA, conducted its investigation, and left without a word to the Rector. Can anyone imagine any such thing happening in a civilised society? Can any panel come into an institution and posit an action that can be considered legally valid without informing the Chief Executive of its arrival?

Nevertheless, this panel was headed by an Archbishop and one of its premier members was a Judge of the Supreme Court of Nigeria. They finished their work and wrote their report without a word to or from the Rector. It was only because of the outcry of the Rector that the panel returned to interview the Rector. Was it not a window dressing? Despite that, all accounts had been studied, approved by the Finance Committee of Council, approved and signed by Council and distributed to all AECAWA and all funding agencies. The panel recommended that all the audited and approved accounts be audited a second time.

It also recommended that since the Rector had been approved for sabbatical leave to take effect at the end of the academic year, and because he could tamper with documents before then, he should be made to relinquish office immediately. That means, based on suspicion only, and without offence, guilt or crime, he should be given the maximum punishment and be publicly disgraced from office as though he was a condemned and notorious criminal.

Incidentally, Rome decided to send her own independent panel, headed by His Eminence, Christian Cardinal Tumi of Douala, Cameroun and two officials from Rome. They had access to all the relevant documents and examined CIWA in all its ramifications, paying special attention to finance. To the greater glory of God, they praised CIWA's administration and academics and concluded that her financial accounting was impeccable.

3.8 PD Akpunonu and AECAWA Presence in CIWA

In his years in CIWA, AECAWA's presence was remarkably felt. Regular governing council meetings took place and were very well attended from across the entire then AECAWA sub-region.

In his days, Fr. Dr. Joseph Amissah (Ghana), the first Registrar of CIWA, who finished his tenure and left, came back to CIWA to join the teaching staff in the Pastoral department and later became the Deputy Rector to PD. In the Biblical department, one had such experts in biblical languages in Kris Owanof Ogoja Diocese, Fr. Dr. Affih Mensa (Ghana) who was also the Dean of Students Affairs. In the Moral department, there was the Alphonsiana, Rome, Fr. Dr. Seth Adom-Oware (Ghana) who was for a very long time in charge of the CIWA Bookshop, which today has metamorphosed into St. Paul's Bookshop in CIWA.

There were practically three or four students each from the other AECAWA sub-gegion in every department of Biblical, Systematic Theology, Moral, Pastoral Theology, Canon Law, and Sacred Liturgy. These students fully integrated themselves with the Nigerian students and culture which gave rise to Wednesday departmental liturgical celebrations aimed at enriching the worship with the various cultural values and genius of these varieties from cultural diversities.

3.9 PD Akpunonu and MISSIO Aachen, Germany

The presence of the late Rev. Prof. Ludwig Bertsch SJ, in the departments of Academic Research and African Projects in missio Aachen, Germany broadened the scope of friendship and support for the CIWA. Through their representatives, MISSIO visited CIWA very often in the years of PD Akpunonu. They visited for various reasons. missio kept its word to give PD whom they literally uprooted from Bigard to CIWA its maximum financial support. With PD Akpunonu, it was necessary for them not only to rely on the written paper progress reports given to them, but to come down physically to see things for themselves. They were never disappointed.

Their conviction each time attracted more funds from them for CIWA's speedy development because the administration was transparently accountable and had concrete evidence to show for their financial commitment to develop CIWA. This explains why in the small space of time, PD was able to transform Obehie tremendously. Rev. Fr. Dr. Anthony Asoanya of Onitsha Archdiocese and late Fr. Simon Kabirat of Kafanchan Diocece who were Directors of Works then bore the burden of erecting those structures.

3.10 PD Akpunonu and the Congregation for the Evangelization of the Peoples and *Opus Sancti Petri*, Rome

The presence of these two offices in Rome was very much felt in the regime of PD Akpunonu. These two did not shirk their responsibilities to CIWA because of the enormous financial assistance coming from MISSIO. Rather they maintained their regular support to CIWA in terms of scholarship awards and for some of the running costs of the Institute. The most striking presence of these offices is felt in the bulky Mass stipends that cushioned the paltry monthly stipends (salary) of the priest members of staff. Thus, each time PD travelled to Rome, the priests both staff and students expected what was popularly called a "windfall." The critical situation was the plight of the female religious members of staff and non-cleric members of staff. How would their monthly stipend be cushioned? If one talked of Mass Stipend, could one talk of Rosary Stipend? PD. Akpunonu had a mysterious way of taking care of these people and still carried everyone along. It can be recalled that in 1990, PD Akpunonu gradually introduced the University

Salary Scale (USS) into CIWA. The bursary department to date has all these details available for confirmation.

Going down memory lane, one could rightly recall once or twice some delegates came from one of these funding agencies. For instance, Msgr. Bernard Prince, to be precise, came to see the management of the finances of CIWA personally. He was said to have been satisfied and pledged to continue to support CIWA.

3.11 PD Akpunonu and Students' Academic/Social Welfare

In his regime, students' academic and social welfare soared very high. At academic defences, he would be physically present and literally chaired all the sessions. Every student that defended received his intervention either as corrections, input, or enrichment of the work. The catholicity of the theses was thus guaranteed. Sports and other social events received good attention, because he believed in *mens sana in corpora sano* – a healthy mind dwells in a healthy body.

3.12 PD Akpunonu and the Development of CIWA Chaplaincy

CIWA to date has the greatest concentration of priests within the sub-region, because most of the students and lecturers are priests. Secondly, CIWA has the largest space both for worship and parking in the whole Port Harcourt municipality. That gives a wonderful variety in the priestly ministries, especially the celebration of the Eucharist and quality homily. The convenience of a large space also attracted many worshippers to CIWA.

From its inception in 1981 until 1991 what is today known, as CIWA Chaplaincy, was a small worshipping community made up of the students of CIWA and a few people who were coming to CIWA for Mass and other religious activities. The group was so small that the chapel for both Sunday and morning Masses was the small place used later by the Centre for the Study of African Culture and Communication (CESACC) for their studio.

The second stage of the development of the chaplaincy was initiated in 1991 by Rev. Fr. Ignatius Obinwa.[13] He was still a student then, and he

---

13 Joe Eboh, ed, *The Making of CIWA Chaplaincy: Our Lady of the Holy Rosary*, p. 33.

announced to that small congregation that he was ready to hold evening instruction every Sunday for those interested in knowing more about the Bible. A good number of those people coming from outside CIWA turned up and he started holding the Bible study sessions with them every Sunday evening. As he was about to graduate and leave CIWA in 1992, those people expressed deep concern over their having to eventually disperse after he left. Although Fr. Camillus Umoh (another student then, but now a Bishop), showed some interest and came sometimes, he was also to graduate and leave CIWA.

Fr. Obinwa thought about the sustainability of the Bible study sessions on Sunday evenings. He decided to get some members of the staff interested in the group. He therefore appealed to Msgr. Hilary Okeke (now the Bishop of Nnewi) to give a talk to the group and he did so. He also appealed to Rev. Fr. J. Brookman-Amissah, a Ghanaian and a lecturer then, to talk to them and he did it. The two were told the reason for inviting them and they showed understanding. So, when Fr. Obinwa left CIWA in 1992, Fr. Amissah, who had got some charismatic orientation in Ghana, took over the group and changed them from a Bible study group to a charismatic group and it started attracting many more people from nearby parishes who were coming to CIWA for charismatic prayers on Sundays and Wednesdays. Many of those people naturally came also for Masses and thus grew CIWA's worshipping community. The group got so swollen with members that the small chapel could no longer contain them and so canopies were made available and spread outside for Masses and charismatic prayer meetings.

The third stage was that of building the multi-purpose hall that now serves as the Chaplaincy Church. Part of the worshipping community grew into a fellowship group that was later renamed St. Paul's Catholic Charismatic Renewal which kept bringing more and more people to CIWA. Because of the increasing number and the inconveniences suffered during rainy season, when some people under the canopies were partially drenched due to rain and wind, the idea of building a multi-purpose hall came up.

The CIWA worshipping community made a formal request to CIWA authorities to build the Multi-Purpose Hall which would cater for the spiritual exercises, the annual CIWA Theology Week, and other conferences and gatherings. The application was made to the then Rector, PD Akpunonu, on September 27, 1994. The permission was granted by the CIWA Governing

Council, and on February 19, 1995, the building committee was inaugu-
rated and funds began to be raised. The building project started shortly after
and was roofed in 1996. Msgr. Hilary Okeke was the Chaplain at that time
and was assisted by the Fr. Ignatius Obinwa who had returned to CIWA, to
serve as an Assistant Lecturer from the 1992/1993 academic year to 1995.
    On Pentecost Sunday, 1996, the Multi-Purpose Hall was first used for
Sunday Mass under Rev. Fr. Patrick C. Chibuko as the Chaplain and assisted by Rev. Fr. Brookman Amissah. The teaming worshippers were provided with spiritual services which included a daily Eucharistic celebration,
a weekly Sacrament of Reconciliation, and the celebration of the Easter
Sacred Triduum. The then Catholic Apostolic Administrator of Port Harcourt, Most Rev. Edmund Fitzgibbon, gave approval for all these and even
permitted CIWA to hold annual harvest and bazaar sales and to keep the
proceeds. These and all the other incomes from the then CIWA chaplaincy
were kept by CIWA and reported to the CIWA Governing Council as in-
ternally generated income.
    It was while the Multi-Purpose Hall was being erected that the Worship-
ping Community applied to the CIWA Senate to be raised to the status
of a Chaplaincy. This was tabled before the Governing Council, and the
approval was given. The Chaplaincy was also to serve as the *Practicum* of
CIWA where the teachers and students would implement what was learned
in the classroom and also improve on their pastoral ministries.
    The Chaplaincy had a turbulent period. The turbulent period was
marked by unguarded excesses and un-Catholic activities by some of the
members of the fellowship group. What started as a Sunday Bible class in
the evening grew into a big crowd of men and women from within and
outside Port Harcourt into a fellowship group. Some of them, for instance,
felt that their fellowship was quite a different phenomenon with its own
dynamics and therefore would not be guided by the CBCN approved format
for the Catholic charismatic renewal. Furthermore, with the erection of the
Chaplaincy, some other problems arose regarding the status and activities
of the Chaplaincy. These issues were not only considered inimical but a
betrayal to the raison d'être of CIWA.
    It was at this period that Rev. Fr. Patrick C. Chibuko was nominated as
Chaplain by the then Rector, Rev. Fr. P. D. Akpunonu and appointed by
Bishop A. O. Makozi in 1995/6–1997 to ensure that authentic Catholic

doctrines were taught in the Chaplaincy and to contain the excesses of some members of the fellowship group who were opposed to Marian practices. The current name of the fellowship group, St. Paul's Charismatic Renewal, tallies with CBCN regulation. It now operates under the Chaplaincy named Our Lady of the Holy Rosary. To emphasise the Catholic orientation of the Chaplaincy, a gigantic statue of Our Lady sponsored by Engr. Joseph Enweluzor and family were erected and serves as evident witness of the successful outcome of the struggle.

Formalizing his position in a document released on March 20, 1996, Bishop A.O. Makozi stated, "The Catholic Institute of West Africa, Port Harcourt, should have a normal Catholic chaplaincy in line with what exists in Nigerian Universities and other higher or tertiary institutions in Nigeria under the competence or jurisdiction of the Ordinary or Bishop of Port Harcourt." The Bishop stated further: "The Chaplain of CIWA should be according to the norms of the laws of the Church [cf. CC. 564–572]. Art 43 par 1 of CIWA Statutes which stipulates that the chaplain shall be appointed by the Governing Council needs to be amended accordingly. The appointment of a chaplain shall be made after consultation with CIWA and the Governing Council."

Meanwhile, the practice of CIWA keeping all the proceeds from the Chaplaincy was initially undisputed during the time of Bishop Makozi. It was seen by all that CIWA needed financial support and the Chaplaincy was seen as one of the avenues for such support. There was also the understanding that CIWA kept the revenue as extra contribution of the diocese of Port Harcourt for playing host to the Institute and in recognition for the many pastoral services rendered by priests staff and students to the local Church. But the continued increase of worshippers and revenue gradually raised some problems regarding the management of the proceeds of the Chaplaincy.

3.13 Two Panels of Enquiry to Probe PD Akpunonu

Like the psalmist would say, "many are the trials of the just man but from them all, the Lord set him free" (Ps 34:19). A local quote has it that when a child succeeds more than his mates in an adventure, the mates call him/her a name in contempt. If a child fetches much better firewood than his mates, the mates would say he collected the wood from the evil forest. When a strong hand cuts the *iroko* tree, it looks as if *iroko* cutting is very light. At the end of PD's second term in office, tongues began to wag and very wildly too, originating from varied quarters especially where they were least expected. Suspicions began from both within and outside CIWA that he was to account for all the finances made available to him.

Incidentally, some prominent individuals behind these probes have died; others are terribly sick or severely physically challenged. Since nothing incriminating came out of them, some have had the humility to meet PD Akpunonu in private to apologise for their lack of sufficient knowledge in passing false incriminating judgment on him. However, they lacked the courage to apologise to him in public, as public insult should demand a public apology.

4. PD Akpunonu on Sabathical Leave in Mundelein

The best thing that has happened to the Seminary – University of Mundelein was to have PD Akpunonu on its staff for one year, as testified by its students. When one sees a rose flower, the first reaction is usually to pluck and keep it. The staff and students of Mundelein felt the same way and followed it up. A representation of this testimony was passed onto the administration that linked up with Akpunonu's local Ordinary. His local Ordinary, incidentally, was on visit to the same university at the time and the deal was struck, signed, and sealed that he should stay much longer in Mundelein. From 1998 until 2014, he was on the academic staff of Mundelein to the joy and edification of all those who came into contact with him. During this period, he constantly took the biblical students for months of academic excursions to Israel.

5. PD Akpunonu now in IweneTansi Major Seminary, Onitsha

PD believes in the principle that home is the best. With all his experiences in Europe and America after all these years, nostalgia made him return permanently to his Archdiocese of Onitsha with the conviction that from here, he could conveniently access Europe and America for a short duration. The seminarians of Iwene Tansi seminary are continuing the laudable refrain of the seminarian students of Mundelein, in having Professor Akpunonu on the seat of Biblical Theology and Exegesis. From Onitsha, PD would willingly access others major Seminaries in where he earlier administered to as Rector in Bigard Memorial Seminary Enugu, namely, the Old Onitsha Ecclesiastical Province which currently includes Calabar, Onitsha and Owerri, Provinces and even beyond.

6. PD Akpunonu as a Scholar

Not to be overlooked is PD's excellent scholarship. PD has published influential volumes on biblical scholarship. Apart from his numerous well researched conference papers and articles published in reputable national and international journals, let us at this juncture bring forward excerpts from two of his books.

6.1 The Overture of the Book of Consolations (Isaiah 40:1–11)

This masterpiece remains an inspiration to writers, musicians, and mystics. The Overture of the Book of Consolations summarises and highlights all the major themes of Deutero-Isaiah. Its predominant theme is consolation – consolation of Israel after the destruction of Jerusalem and the temple and the depopulation of the kingdom of Judah. The Overture assures Judah that the past is forgiven and Yahweh is ushering in a New Creation, a future more glorious than the Exodus, the march through the desert, where Israel will once again be wedded to her husband: Yahweh, the Holy One of Israel.[14]

6.2 The Vine, Israel and the Church

The vine is one of the blessings of the Promised Land. Since Israel is precious in the eyes of Yahweh, she is also called the vine. But this vine was a failure in some prophetic and wisdom writings. The metaphor was taken over in the New Testament where the Kingdom of Heaven was compared to the vine but with this marked difference: this vine was to bear lasting

---

14 Peter Damian Akpunonu *The Overture of the Book of Consolations (Isaiah 40:1–11)* Peter Lang, 2004, 116 pages.

fruit. This is so because Jesus is the true vine, and his salvific work is carried on in His Church.[15]

These two books symbolise a comprehensive collection of ground breaking works from one of the principal figures in biblical exegesis. The essence of a good teacher is that he will lead his students into a realization of his own mind. I believe that these two books did just that. As you read these works, I pray that you realize what a remarkable man the author is and how God used him for His glory. They are "a must-read" for all who are interested and enjoy reading inspirational works and summarised research.

7. Final Reflections

PD Akpunonu put the greatest parts of his genius into his teaching, administration, and research. Talk of an exemplary teacher, he is one; talk of an able administrator, he is one. Talk of an ideal scholar he is equally one. He is someone who gets on well with the youths and that explains why he remains always youthful in every aspect, especially mentally and physically. For him every aspect of the life of a priest must be tip-top, especially in the liturgy. Only the best is good enough in worship beginning from the elaborate preparations, edifying celebration in an admirable decorum.

There is this one little thing one has questions about. Everyone has his or her impish side. After PD's regime, the question still remains, to what extent has CIWA taxied during his administration? In as much as one would love to leave posterity to judge, one could rightly underscore the fact that during his regime, CIWA not only taxied but also went airborne like A 380 Airbus jet airliner with an original three class configuration of eight hundred and fifty three passengers and cruised freely at the speed of about one thousand kilometers per hour at the high altitude of about thirty nine thousand feet above sea level. With PD in the cockpit as the pilot and ably assisted by co-pilots, flight engineers, and other crew attendants, the airbus landed safely in 1997 although not without challenges which were aptly and carefully handled.

---

15 Peter Damian Akpunonu, *The Vine, Israel and the Church, Frankfurt a. m:* Peter Lang, 2004, 228 pages.

The clear evidence of this success on the pages of this Festschrift lends credible support to this claim. And so by way of illustration, it became obvious that with the acquisition of land at Obehie and its speedy and massive development by PD, it was possible for the CBCN to have a start-off campus for the laudable and enviable establishment of *Veritas* University, Abuja.

CIWA could have metamorphosed into CUWA and would be competing with its contemporary ecclesiastical counterparts in Africa if PD Akpunonu had his way. CIWA still has a chance, even to re-acquire Ozuoba. CIWA should never lose sight of being an AECAWA affair and this should give it an edge in any matter even on national issues. We are grateful for the life and ministry of PD, and hope that this Festschrift in some small way expresses our appreciation and admiration for him and the contributions he has made to improve the lives of thousands of students, seminarians, priests, religious women and men, as well as the members of the laity through his teaching, research, and preaching ministries in the West African Sub-Region and beyond.

PD Akpunonu remains an active member of the Catholic Biblical Association of America; a member of the Conference of Catholic Theological Institutions; a member of the Ecumenical Association of Third World Theologians. He was also a papal delegate to the Twelfth Ordinary Synod of Bishops held between October 5–28, 2008 on The Word of God in the Life and Mission of the Church. One feels ever richer for having known PD Akpunonu.

8. Conclusion

What we have put down on the pages of this Festschrift represents our views on the man PD Akpunonu and his quality administration in the two institutions: Bigard Seminary, Enugu and Catholic Institute of West Africa, Port Harcourt. It was not our intention to present a martyr to be pitied or a saint to be venerated but rather to present a man of God, who responded wholeheartedly to God's call as a priest, human frailties notwithstanding. We present a man who knew the value of availability and made it his second nature. He simply made himself available, his talents and time and aptly applied them to the best of his ability in the Lord's ministry especially in the areas of formation, teaching, and research. This is exactly what this

Festschrift is out to testify to in very clear terms. We present a man who has the basic good will to do good to everyone, especially when he is carried along with truth, honesty, and transparency. With these virtues, he would go to any length to defend and save vocations. These rare virtues also influenced his administration a great deal.

We would not have covered all that needed to be said about PD Akpunonu and his administration in the two Institutions. We would not claim to be flawless in the presentation of our details on this "role model" and "icon of no mean repute." But note that, other contributors to this Festschrift would be able to cover what might be lacking in our own presentation for we simply presented PD and his administration the way "we saw it." We simply attempted to inform as best as we could, while admitting that any form of misrepresentation would be well and humbly acknowledged.

Finally, how do we judge PD Akpunonu and his regime in the two Institutions? How do we objectively assess his quality-result-oriented administration in the two Institutions? What marks do we award the unprecedented and second to none here-after administration of PD Akpunonu? Our people have a saying that, "if you say a car is good," the next question to ask would be, "whether it is as good as Mercedes." Hitherto, as far as these two Institutions were concerned, what could prevent PD Akpunonu from fitting perfectly into this saying? Furthermore, without pre-empting the objective assessment and judgement of posterity and even the worst critics of PD Akpunonu and his administration in these duo Institutions, and given his laudable and eloquent achievements, could anyone or anything prevent scoring him *Summa Cum Laude Probatus* with Superlative *Aggregate*? Let time and history pronounce the verdict.

Matthew Obiekezie

Peter Damian Akpunonu: Rector in Catholic Institute of West Africa and Ecclesiastical Ambassador in United States

1. Introduction

In the throes of Fr. Peter Damian's (PD) departure to the United States on June 22, 1997, a member of the Catholic Institute of West Africa (CIWA) faculty wrote to the Deputy Rector on 16 July 1997:

> There is nothing hidden which will not be revealed. If anybody thinks he or she has a case against anyone, let the person bring it up in the open, applying "appropriate procedures," and we will settle it as God's children. If I am at fault, I will apologize for it and try to make amends to the best of my ability. Hopefully we will all do the same. But as for this underground and underhand subversive activity, it is not worthy of our calling as anointed and consecrated people. If I have to die for saying openly what we all know, then let me die for it, provided that the truth triumphs and darkness is put to flight. I think that enough is enough of secret meetings, subversive activities, damaging cliques and secret, incriminating letters in CIWA, sometimes written for others to sign.

The departure to, and the sojourn of Fr. Peter Damian in the United States of America cannot be adequately discussed without a preface to the story. The above-cited lamentation was a belated disavowal of the shocking situation that prevailed among the members of the senior staff in CIWA during and after Fr. PD's tenure as Rector of CIWA.

2. Eight Years of Leadership in CIWA: Success in spite of man-made challenges

Fr. PD assumed office as the Rector of CIWA in the fall of 1989, a post he held until June 20, 1997. His qualification for this office abundantly spoke for itself. Before his rectorship of CIWA, Fr. PD was training priests for a quarter of a century at the Bigard Memorial Seminary Enugu (1972–1997). He was Lecturer of Sacred Scriptures and Hebrew (1972–1978), the

Academic Dean of the Faculty of Theology (1974–1977), the Vice Rector of Bigard Memorial Seminary (1977–1978), and the Rector of Bigard Memorial Seminary, Enugu (1979–1989). His poise, energy, and academic brilliance abundantly equipped him for the noblest work of preparing priests for the service of God in the South Eastern Nigeria, including a little bit of the Cameroons, and Sierra Leone. No wonder he was found to be the best hand to move forward the affairs of a struggling CIWA, a tertiary institution embracing the entire English-speaking West African Catholic dioceses. All those who passed through Fr. PD's formation will testify to a rare combination of genuine spirituality and academic thoroughness. His sharp focus on his work had always guaranteed success, but this does not shield him from envy.

Once in CIWA, Fr. PD sought to introduce an academic leadership that bespoke the dignity of the priesthood and the first tertiary ecclesiastical institution in the West African Sub-Region. He had to work with some faculty members and priests that he did not know before or had not trained, and priests from other regions or seminaries in Nigeria, Ghana, and the Sierra Leone. Some members of the academic and administrative staff came from various parts of Nigeria, each carrying its own tribal sentiments and prejudices that are characteristic of Nigerians. Here you have a community of priests with different expectations, and who are tough to please. CIWA was growing and Fr. PD had to provide leadership.

However, Fr. PD first had to dismantle the developmental impasse created by the difficulty of Port Harcourt diocese in providing adequate land for the development of CIWA. The Catholic diocese of Port Harcourt had already given a rectory and another piece of property for CIWA. However, CIWA could not reach its full potential, being sited on such an obviously insufficient property. When it stalled for too long to acquire additional land for CIWA from the diocese of Port Harcourt, Fr. Peter Damian had to request for land from a nearby diocese of Aba. An adequate piece of land was found in Obehie, Asa, and was approved by the owners of CIWA. An approval was granted by CIWA's Governing Council for work to start immediately on the new site. This brave move by Fr. Peter Damian to search for and to acquire additional land for CIWA outside the Port Harcourt diocese provoked the ire of the Catholic leadership of the host diocese of Port Harcourt, who felt that CIWA was being moved away from the diocese. This new land acquisition once and for all complicated the relationship between the Ordinary of Port Harcourt and the Rector of CIWA. It was even feared that this tense situation was beginning to influence some of the clergy of the Port Harcourt diocese. It would appear that collegiality among bishops promotes complacency and makes them turn a blind eye to some issues. However, the Obehie campus was and continues to be a monumental achievement for CIWA. It was discouraging to deny the Rector of CIWA the support he needed for the marvelous job that he was doing. Even so, Fr. Peter Damian remained undeterred, though sad to say that all those who knew the truth of the controversies of CIWA decided to remain aloof.

However, Fr. PD had visions and was determined to make a difference in CIWA. In a very short amount of time, he began to develop the Obehie campus and in a space of one calendar year contracted a simultaneous development of 26 buildings in the Obehie campus of CIWA. It was mind boggling to learn that some people were not happy to see CIWA develop in Aba diocese. Hence the so-called talk about "simultaneous development" of Port Harcourt and Obehie campuses. Rather, it would appear that the problem was that Fr. PD made success too quickly in a matter that had stunted for a long time. A blanket protest was that CIWA was being moved from Port Harcourt diocese.

Fr. Peter Damian knew how to raise funds. It was difficult for the funding agencies to deny him help, because it was abundantly evident that he was judiciously using the funds as requested. The funding agencies never complained. Truly, Fr. PD raised a lot of funds to run and develop CIWA. Someone ridiculously said, "If he put so much in the running and development of CIWA, how much has he embezzled?" CIWA Statutes mandate an annual audit of all CIWA finances. The auditing of CIWA finances was timely done every year of Fr. Peter Damian's rectorship. The funding agencies demanded their experts to review the accounts before a new approval of funds. In fact, the funding agencies had often sent their auditors to CIWA to verify the accounts of CIWA. This verification was a standard practice. The accounts' records always passed.

At a time, some of the members of the CIWA Governing Council demanded a twice monthly inspection of the CIWA accounts. They never found a problem. Then, some of the members of the council instigated that CIWA accounts be audited from five years back. One would assume that if expert auditing was correct every year of the five years, it must be correct in the five years put together – a simple mathematical truth. Yet, the chairman of the governing council allowed a lot of money to be paid to a famous auditing firm for a five-year audit of the CIWA accounts. No problems were ever found. As a result of the simultaneous erection of the academic, administrative, and residential buildings in the Obehie campus, and the running of the programs of CIWA in the Port Harcourt campus, no amount of money was sufficient. Yet, some dioceses would not even pay their normal agreed upon contributions for CIWA educational programs. The reason for this passivity was difficult to know, perhaps, either to make administration difficult for CIWA or to slow Fr. Peter Damian down, but CIWA continued to develop. The question was: Why does he succeed? How does he find funds? Once, some important member of the governing council forgot his facts and complained that Fr. PD did not even ask for permission before requesting help from the funding agencies. Written correspondences between the accuser and the accused came in favour of Fr. PD; *verba volant, scripta manent.*

Even among the student priests, some students would transfer the aggression arising from frustrations coming from their home dioceses onto the administration of CIWA. In order to help the students of CIWA, Fr. PD would request Mass stipends from overseas benefactors and distributed the funds to priests on the staff of CIWA and to priest-students of CIWA. The distribution of Mass stipends usually created momentary joys, but everyone soon went back to their clandestine and clannish loyalties.

It must be noted that through his eight years tenure as Rector of CIWA, the academic programs were undisturbed, the campus life was peaceful, and the priest-students enjoyed adequate peace. Just as the cited paragraph above, some members of the senior staff remained mired in clandestine meetings, malicious mendacity, and envy. Despite the bickering of some members of the senior staff, Fr. Peter Damian was in good control of the senior staff of CIWA. He did not introduce personal insatiateness to some members of the senior staff. The power of the Rector by statutes is not unrestricted. Those who could help correct matters either thought, "Provided it's not me;" or they were a part of the problem. Fr. Peter Damian is a perfect gentleman. The lot of the gentle is not always easy. He left CIWA undaunted.

3. Ecclesiastical Ambassador in US

According to the Statutes of CIWA, after a second term as the Rector of CIWA, Fr. PD was bound to relinquish the office of the Rector of CIWA to another appointee of the Governing Council of CIWA. He was eligible for a sabbatical leave for which he applied, and received approval to leave in July 1997. But a group in the governing council of CIWA insisted on his leaving office in the last week of June 1997, in pretext that he could "tamper" with some documents in his office if he was left to stay until July, as some investigation was already ordered to take place. This marginal victory was too late and made little sense. Fr. Peter Damian humbly accepted the humiliation of ingratitude and moved onto the United States of America where he reinvented himself.

Fr. Peter Damian built his résumé on 25 years of teaching and forming priests and seminarians in Nigeria. His reputation and integrity in this field remained impeccable and unrivalled. As an administrator of Bigard Memorial Seminary and CIWA, Fr. Peter Damian continued to find time to prepare and to teach students every semester. He had always wished that he found time for more academic work. He contributed to several outstanding journals. He never flaunted his successes, but he was a gold medalist of his Pontifical Urban University, Rome (1965).

In the United States, he hoped to teach at the Catholic Theological University (CTU), Chicago, but this arrangement failed. In October 1997, he was hired by the University of St. Mary of the Lake (USML), Mundelein, Illinois, as Adjunct Professor of Exegesis, Old and New Testaments. The University of St. Mary of the Lake, the very first university of the State of Illinois, is also a regional seminary owned by the archdiocese of Chicago. To teach seminarians is Fr. Peter Damian's second nature. The faculty and students soon discovered in Fr. Peter Damian a brilliant gem and an experienced priest-trainer in their midst. Fr. Peter Damian's sabbatical leave was supposed to end, but the university was not finished with him. In 1999, Fr. Peter Damian was promoted to full Professor of Exegesis, Old and New Testament.

Fr. Peter Damian's lectures sold out. Students and faculty commended him. He taught courses in Isaiah, Jeremiah, Ezekiel, Daniel, and the Books of Samuel. In the New Testament, he taught courses in Epistle to the

Hebrews, the Acts of the Apostles, and Epistle to the Galatians. He taught four courses each semester. Fr. PD's lectures on the Epistle to the Hebrews and the Prophet Isaiah were each four hours a week.

One other major thing Fr. Peter Damian did for the USML was to lead their students to the Holy Land every year in the fall for eight weeks. Later, this pilgrimage was directed to Turkey, Greece, and Rome, because of the Palestinian "intifada" (uprising). During this pilgrimage named, "In the Footsteps of Saint Paul," normal classes were held. Fr. PD looked forward every year to leading very enthusiastic and excited students to discover the roots of Christianity and the Holy Scriptures. At a time when someone else shared leading the students on this academic pilgrimage, some of the students thought it was not the same experience. The pilgrimage experience sharpened even more Fr. PD's expertise on the Holy Scripture, and one could not help being "wowed" whenever he opened his mouth in matters concerning the Christian Bible. The students openly stated that no student should ever pass through St. Mary of the Lake University without doing some course work with Fr. Peter Damian.

After the fifth year with the USML, Francis Cardinal George wrote the late Archbishop of Onitsha to extend the stay of Fr. PD. His role in the institution was admirable and appreciated. It is not accurate to imagine that Fr. PD found life comfortable in the United States and was reluctant to return home. The truth of the matter is that after five years, when he wanted to return home for good, the then Ordinary asked him to defer it. Even after many years at Mundelein, when Fr. PD decided finally to return home, the present Rector/President of the University of Mundelein asked Archbishop Valerian Okeke to permit PD give more time to Mundelein. Fr. PD's good works invariably attracted gifts of books and other things from Mundelein for the seminary in Onitsha. About 85% of the books at Tansi Seminary were donated to the seminary, because of Fr. PD.

During his stay in Mundelein, Fr. PD carried out a weekend ministry at St. John the Evangelist Church, Streamwood, Illinois. During his summer vacations, he was usually invited to give lectures and conferences on various books of the Holy Scriptures to a regular group of parishioners at the Church of the Maternity of the Blessed Virgin Mary, Philadelphia, Pennsylvania. He also led that parish on pilgrimage to the Holy Land in the summer of 2013. The people who discovered Fr. PD in the United

States used the opportunity to get everything possible they could get from him. Though an African, Fr. Peter Damian was appointed one of the experts of the Church at the General Synod of the Word of God in the Life and Ministry of the Church (2008). During his stay in the United States of America, Fr. PD was appointed a member of International Theological Commission (2004–2013). In this commission, he collaborated in the writing of the following documents: The hope of salvation for infants who die without baptism (2007); The search of universal ethics: A new look at the natural law (2009); Theology today: Perspectives, principles, and criteria (2012). Other documents include: God the Trinity and the unity of humanity: Christian monotheism and its opposition to violence (2012), and Sensus fidei in the life of the Church (2012). In all that happened in these sixteen years sojourn outside Nigeria, Fr. Peter Damian has shown himself a good ambassador of our local Nigerian Church to the Catholic Church in the United States of America.

Fr. Peter Damian was happy in 2004 to publish two of his original works: The Vine, Israel and the Church (2004), The Overture of the Book of Consolations (2004). His latest publication was: In the Footsteps of St. Paul (2015). On a rather personal note, Fr. PD visited his ageing mother every year in December for a few days before leaving for pilgrimage with his students. During his visits to Nigeria, he made his annual reunion with the Archbishop of Onitsha, his bishop, and touched base with home and friends.

4. Conclusion

I am happy for the opportunity to contribute to this write-up to celebrate the Golden Jubilee of Fr. Peter Damian's priestly ordination. I thought that it was necessary to preface the story of Fr. PD's stay in the United States of America with a euphemistic episode of the situation at CIWA from 1989 to 1997. I was a student of CIWA from 1990 to 1992. I was a member of the senior staff of CIWA from 1995 to 1997. The first question I asked Fr. Peter Damian before writing this article was: Why did you go to the United States of America after CIWA? His answer was: to get to my brother Dama (Damasus), just to get some rest. Some of the routine meetings of CIWA during his tenure as Rector can be said to be unfriendly, if not outright brutal. People who met Fr. Peter Damian have always respected him very much. To see Fr. Peter Damian suffer at the hands of people one expected to understand the meaning of justice and fair play was disheartening.

Fr. PD is a happy man. He survived CIWA and he is healthy and happy. He has always trusted in the vindication of God and he remained prayerful. He has no malice; he has no enemy. His former students love, respect, and support him. In the summer of 1998, some priests studying in Germany heard that Fr. Peter Damian was visiting Germany. The students quickly rallied around in the residence of one of the priests to receive him. Everyone who visited that occasion said encouraging words to him. When Fr. Peter Damian was about to return to Nigeria from the United States on July 19, 2013, some priests and religious rallied around again to organise a befitting farewell they tagged "Celebrating a Legend." The occasion attracted a huge crowd, as people attended from various states in the United States. The Archbishop of Onitsha showed his generous side, as he welcomed Fr. PD with style, giving him a respectful residence and promised to do whatever it takes to take care of him. On coming home, some of Fr. PD's former students organised a big "Welcome Back Home" to show PD how much he is loved, respected, and appreciated. Fr. Peter Damian resides near the Iwene Tansi Seminary and has naturally continued his God-given role of teaching and preparing priests for their role in our Church and society.

Ignatius M. C. Obinwa

The Biblical and African Orientations to Leadership

1. Preamble

It is my heartfelt pleasure to write this brief overview on the concept of leadership in the Old Testament. Not only is it my favourite topic, but also because I am writing it in honour of a person who is dear to me. My former Rector and Lecturer, the Very Rev. Fr. Prof. Peter Damian Akpunonu. He is also a person who is personally versed in Old Testament Studies and has attained the academic rank of Professor of Old Testament. He has equally shown himself to be an accomplished leader. For instance, he was a long-lasting Rector of a national institution; the *Bigard Memorial Seminary, Enugu, Nigeria* and also an international one; the *Catholic Institute of West Africa (CIWA), Port Harcourt, Nigeria*, and he exhibited very high leadership qualities in both of them. I am elated to dedicate this study to him as he marks his sacerdotal Golden Jubilee.

2. Introduction

The term "Old Testament", which serves as the title of the first part of the Christian Bible, literally means *Old Covenant (palaia diathēkē*, cf. 2 Cor 3:14). It is the opposite or parallel term to *New Testament* which is the name given to the second part of the Christian Bible, and it literally means *New Covenant (kaine diathēkē*, cf. Jer 38:31; 2 Cor 3:6 and Heb Jer 31:31). The *Old Testament* is indeed the Bible of the Jews, being the religious-historical record of the very lengthy divine-human interactions between God (Yahweh) and the ancient people of Israel. According to biblical re-cords, the interactions began with the story of their great ancestor Abraham (Gen 12:1ff) but became sharpened when Yahweh revealed himself to the people through Moses (cf. Exod 3:1–22). Moses became then the people's first visible or human leader[1] through whose instrumentality Yahweh later adopted them as his special people by means of the covenant he made with them on Mount Sinai (cf. Exod 19:10–20:1–17). Studying the concept of leadership in the Old Testament is, therefore, tantamount to studying the political history of Israel, which is cast on a religious platform, because the nucleus of it is the mentioned divine-human encounter that commences in Genesis 12 and Exodus 3. The aim of this paper is to explore the major aspects of the Israelite leadership and the qualities exhibited by prominent leading personalities in the OT as a means of presenting the contemporary leaders in Africa and in other continents with role models to emulate. We shall therefore examine leadership as a general concept, explore the OT's leadership issues, briefly cast a look at how leadership is practised in Africa and beyond, and then sift out the good aspects of the OT's leadership that can help modern leaders in discharging their duties well.

3. Definition of Leadership

Before delving into the OT's concept of leadership, it is necessary to survey what the term leadership generally means as a basis for searching for its application in the OT or among the ancient people of Israel. Defining leadership is a rather complex issue because, as Cecil A. Gibb rightly notes, "There is a great variety of ways in which one individual stands out from others in social situations and in which the one may be said therefore to be 'leading' the others. So diverse are these ways that any one concept attempting to encompass them all as 'leadership' does lose the specificity and precision that is necessary to scientific thinking."[2] Due to this complexity, scholars have varied descriptions of the term leadership. For instance,

---

1   Yahweh is really the leader of his people. Moses and all the other human leaders of Israel are Yahweh's chosen representatives whom he placed on his *own* throne as his viceroys among the people (cf. 1 Chron 28:5; 29:23; 2 Chron 9:8; 13:8; Ps 110).

2   C. A. Gibb, "Leadership (Psychological Aspect" in: *The International Encyclopedia of the Social Sciences*, Vols. 9/10 (New York: Macmillan) p. 91 cited by O.B.C. Nwolisa, "Models of Leadership: A Theoretical Exploration, with Empirical Comparative Civil-Military Performance," *The Nigerian Journal of Theology*, 1/5 (April 1990) 19.

Daniel I. Block says: "By 'leader' we mean a person who inspires, guides, conducts, or rules others. 'Leadership' denotes the position or office held by a leader."[3] According to M. Chemers, leadership is "a process of social influence in which one person can enlist the aid and support of others in the accomplishment of a common task."[4] Eric Thomas Weber defines good leadership simply as "judicious, yet courageous guidance."[5] One can indeed say that an essential aspect of leadership is the idea of a person (or some persons) exercising influence on the actions and affairs of others or acting as a catalyst in a human society. Generally speaking, leadership means the act of a person or some persons being at the forefront or at the head of others in order to give direction or to show the way. This idea of *leadership* is embedded in the Greek verb *archein* which means "to lead, to rule, to govern or to initiate," as well as in its participle *archōn* which means both *leading* and a *leader*. It is from the same root that the substantive *ho archēgos* comes, and it bears the meaning of: *the first* or *pre-eminent person, i.e., the leader*. Thus leadership involves both being at *the head* (being *the first – hē archē*) and also *initiating* (*archein*) actions, especially the actions which make for the well-being and progress of the led. There is a semantically similar word in Hebrew, *nāśî'* which has such meanings as a *prince*, a *chief* or a *shepherd* in the sense of a *leader* (cf. Num 2:3; Ezek 32:29; 34:23–24).[6] There are other synonymous Greek terms which present the idea of leadership, for instance, the verb *hodēgeō* which means "to lead," "to guide," or literally, "to show the way," as well as the noun *hēgemōn* meaning a *leader* in the

---

3   Daniel I. Block, "Leader, Leadership, OT" in: Katharine Doob Sakenfeld, *et. al.* (eds.), *The New Interpreter's Dictionary of the Bible*, Volume 3 (Nashville: Abingdon Press, 2008) 620.

4   M. Chemers, "An Integrative Theory of Leadership," accessed on 08.06.2014 from: http://en.wikipedia.org/wiki/Leadership#Situational_and_contingency_theories.

5   Eric Thomas Weber, "Leadership is not in conflict with democratic values" accessed from http://www.tehrantimes.com/component/content/article/116733 on 02.07.2014.

6   Cf. David J. A. Clines (ed.), *The Dictionary of Classical Hebrew*, Volume V (Sheffield: Sheffield Academic Press, 2001) 772 und also Wilhelm Gesenius, *Hebräisches und Aramäisches Handwörterbuch über das Alte Testament*, 18. Auflage (Heidelberg: Springer, 2013) 853. The term *qāṣîn* is a synonym for *nāśî'* (cf. Judg 11:6).

sense of a governor (cf. Matt 28:14).[7] In résumé, leadership encapsulates
the idea of someone being at the commanding position, someone having
a special status among a group of people and having the capacity and the
duty of initiating actions or processes.[8] However, leadership can be positive
or negative – positive if the actions and processes initiated are progressive;
leading to the welfare and development of those being led, negative if it is
an exploitative type of leadership; leading to the unnecessary and unwar-
ranted suffering of masses of people.

Since the idea of leading is concomitant with any organised society, the
concept of *leadership* is equally found in every language spoken by any
organised people. For instance, it is found in African languages but due to
their numerousness and the limited space in this write-up, we can simply
take one example – the Igbo language[9] of Nigeria. The substantive used in
Igbo language to mean *leadership* is *odúdú*. It also means *to lead* and *leading* when used as a verb (*infinitive* and *participle* respectively). The Igbo
phrase *ónyè ndù* is used to translate *a leader*. Another Igbo word which
means a *leader* is *onye-isi* (which literally means *someone at the head*). It is a
synonym of the Greek *ho archēgos* (the pre-eminent fellow) and the Hebrew
nāśîʼ (a prince, a chief or a *leader*) mentioned above. The semantic content
of the term *onye-isi* is a person who goes in front of, or goes along with the
person or the people being led, and performs the service of showing the way
or the right direction. It is the work of such a fellow to show a person or a
group of persons passing through an unfamiliar zone how to find the way
to their destination, or to help people who are not very knowledgeable in
a thing how to achieve a desired goal. This shows then that achieving the
desired goal by those being led is dependent on whether the *ónyè ndù* (*a
leader*) is good or not. It behoves a *good leader* (*ézigbo ónyè ndù*) to have
very clear knowledge of the intended goal or the destination (the *terminus*

---

7   The term *hēgemōn* (leading person, chief, governor) is indeed a participle derived
    from the deponent verb *hēgéomai* which means "to lead," "to be chief," or "to
    govern."
8   Cf. Frederick William Danker (ed.), *A Greek-English Lexicon of the New Testa-
    ment and Other Early Christian Literature*, Third Edition (Chicago: The Uni-
    versity of Chicago Press, 2000) 137–140.
9   Igbo is one of the three major languages spoken in Nigeria, in West Africa. The
    other two major Nigerian languages are Hausa and Yoruba.

ad quem), to have at his/her fingertips the easiest and the best means of arriving at that set goal and also to have the good will to take the led to that goal.[10] Indeed, to be a good leader one also needs to be large-hearted, eschew selfishness, be self-sacrificing and generous with one's knowledge, energy, time, and other resources necessary for achieving the desired and set goal which is for the good of all.

4. Leadership in the Old Testament

In the Old Testament, one sees both the positive and the negative aspects of leadership, depending on how the actions of the various Israelite leaders have impacted on the people. It is not feasible in this write-up to mention or describe all who have exercised leadership office in ancient Israel, only a few prominent ones will suffice. For instance, one can think of such figures as Moses, Joshua, Samuel, Saul, David, Solomon, Manasseh, and Josiah.

Moses: Leadership in Israel began with Moses because it was under him that the people were united as a nation. G. O. Abe states "The founding of Israel as 'a nation' would be credited to Moses whose qualifications are tremendous. All charismatic qualities of a true national leader were basic with him."[11] According to a biblical narrative, Moses (*Moshe* in Hebrew) was the name given by an Egyptian princess to a Hebrew child she *drew from water* (cf. Exod 2:10).[12] This child grew up and eventually became the

---

10 An Igbo hymn of confidence says: *Obim atuna ujo, onye n'edu gi maalu uzo* (literally: "Have no fears my soul, your leader [God] knows the way"). This point of *knowing the way* is very important for a leader, hence regarding the Pharisees, *who did not know the way*; who lacked the correct perspectives of what they were teaching, Jesus says: "Let them alone; they are blind guides. And if a blind man leads a blind man, both will fall into a pit" (Matt 15:14).

11 G. O. Abe, "The Old Testament Concept of Leadership Role in Nation Build- ing" in: *African Journal of Biblical Studies (AJBS)*, VI/1 (April, 1991) 30.

12 Pharaoh's daughter named him Moses, for she said, "Because I drew him out of the water" (Exod 2:10). This is based on the popular etymology of the name Moses which is taken to come from the Hebrew verb *mashah* meaning "to draw out," "to save," or "to rescue," cf. Karl Feyerabend, *Langenscheidt's Pocket Hebrew Dictionary to the Old Testament* (Berlin: Langenscheidt, no date) 199. But since the daughter of Pharaoh was not a Jew, the name might rather have Egyptian meaning since there are such Egyptian parallels as Ahmoses (Ahmose/ Ahmesu), Ramoses (Ramses/Ramesu), and Tutmoses (Thutmose) – "the god Tut

leader of the Israelites and the human instrument employed by Yahweh in liberating the Israelite people from their Egyptian bondage (Exod 3:1ff). His leadership qualities were fully tested and proved to be exceptional, because it was in the hardship of wilderness that he had to lead thousands[13] of the Israelites from Egypt to the Promised Land. Due to the normal nature of wilderness, the people lacked water, food and meat, and so they repeatedly complained against Moses, their leader. Possessing the leadership quality of serenity, Moses was able to calm the charged atmosphere by showing concern for the plight of the people and running to God for help in providing the people with the basic necessities they craved. Josephus says,

> But as for Moses himself, while the multitude were irritated and bitterly set against him, he cheerfully relied upon God, and upon his consciousness of the care he had taken of these his own people: and he came into the midst of them, even while they clamored against him, and had stones in their hands in order to dispatch him. Now he was an agreeable presence, and very able to persuade the people by his speeches; accordingly he began to mitigate their anger, and exhorted them not to be over-mindful of their present adversities, lest they should thereby suffer the benefits that had formerly been bestowed on them to slip off their memories... but to expect deliverance out of those their present troubles....[14]

Moses was a humble leader who could listen and accept good advice. Initially Moses was the sole leader, working alone from morning to evening in order to provide instruction and justice for the people. This must surely have made him a very important figure among the people, even though the work was draining. Jethro, his father-in-law, advised him to share the

---

is born," cf. footnote on Exod 2:10 in the *New Jerusalem Bible*, and also G. O. Abe, "The Old Testament Concept of Leadership Role in Nation Building," 31.

13 According to Exod 12:37, "And the people of Israel journeyed from Rameses to Succoth, about six hundred thousand men on foot, besides women and children." If the young men of military age were said to be up to six hundred thousand, then when the old men, the women and the children are reckoned the number would swell to about 2,500.000 as Gottwald suggests. See Norman K. Gottwald, *The Tribes of Yahweh* (Maryknoll, New York: Orbis Books, 1979) 51 and Emmanuel O. Nwaoru, "Leadership Style of Moses in Exodus 15:22–18:27: A Biblical Paradigm for African Leaders," in: Bernard Ukwuegbu *et al* (eds.), *Good Citizenship and Leadership in the Bible* (Port Harcourt: CABAN publications, 2014), 7.

14 *The Works of Josephus, Complete and Unabridged*, New and updated Edition, Book Three, Chapter 1, translated by William Whiston (Peabody, MA: Hendrickson Publishers, 1996) 79.

responsibility with some elders of the people. Taking the advice demanded much humility from him because, though it reduced his work, it also reduced his personal ego and importance among the people. He took the advice and thereby practised a collaborative style of leadership by sharing leadership authority and duties with some elders of Israel (cf. Exod 18:1–27).[15] Moses exhibited a democratic type of leadership by sharing with others both the responsibilities and the honour of belonging to the leadership office. He would not act like a dictator (a *scit omnia*; *Mr.-know-it-all*). Probably, this advice given to Moses by Jethro led Moses to later give the instruction that a leader of the people should not exalt himself above other members of the community. Thus, he summarised the behavioural code for the Israelite leaders in the general instruction he gave during the exodus journey, before the people entered into the Promised Land, saying:

> When you have come into the land that the LORD your God is giving you ... you may indeed set over you a king ... silver and gold he must not acquire in great quantity for himself ... he shall have a copy of this law written.... It shall remain with him and he shall read in it all the days of his life, so that he may learn to fear the LORD his God, diligently observing all the words of this law and these statutes, neither exalting himself above other members of the community nor turning aside from the commandment.... (Deut 17:14–20).

That he should not make heavy acquisitions *for himself* speaks against any form of *selfishness* on the part of a leader. Again, that the king or the leader should not exalt himself above the other members of the community harps on the *humility* that marks a good leader. The instruction seems to have been carried into later communities of the Jews.[16] Thus, with regard to *The Letter of Aristeas* which was addressed to Greek-speaking Jews, Mendels notes:

> In the treatise 'On Kingship' in the Scroll, the king commissions... the captains of thousands, captains of hundreds, captains of fifties and captains of tens (57.3–4)....

---

15 Cf. Mary Jerome Obiorah, "'You Cannot Do It Alone' (Exod 18:18): A Biblical Advice on Collaborative Ministry" in: Ignatius M.C. Obinwa (ed.), *Collaborative Ministry in the Context of Inculturation* (Onitsha, Cameroon: Africana First Publishers, 2006) 35–45.

16 Cf. Doron Mendels, *Identity, Religion and Historiography: Studies in Hellenistic History*, Journal for the Study of the Pseudepigrapha, Supplement Series 24 (England: Sheffield Academic Press, 1998) 326.

The king's council in the Scroll is a judicial council of 36 members (57.11–15) including '12 rulers of the people, 12 priests, and 12 Levites'. These will sit with the king 'for justice and the Law'… and the king's 'heart may not be lifted up above them, and he will do nothing in any counsel without them.'[17]

So, the king/leader must not be haughty in his relationship with his counselors and the other members of the community. That is what the expression in Ezek 34:23–24 that the new *David would be prince among the people* really implies; though placed *above them* (*'ălêhem*) as their shepherd/leader, he would humbly work *among them* (*b^etôkem*) as one of them.[18] The leadership of Moses is then that of humility, collaboration and concern for the well-being of the people being led.

Joshua: After the death of Moses, Joshua took over his leadership role and he also exercised the role creditably. According to Num 13:16, his original name was *Hôshēa'* (Hosea), derived from the root *yāsha'* (to save, deliver) and meaning "salvation." But Moses changed it *Yehôshua'* (Joshua)[19], which is a more complete form of the name, meaning "Yahweh is salvation." It is a name that reminds the people of their deliverance from their Egyptian bondage. The encounter Joshua had with the captain of the spiritual army of Yahweh (cf. Josh 5:13–15) was exactly like what Moses experienced at his own spiritual encounter at the burning bush (Exod 3:1–5); both of them were asked to remove their shoes because they were standing on holy ground; that means to purify themselves because they

---

17 Doron Mendels, *Identity*, 330–331.
18 See I.M.C. Obinwa, *The Shepherd Motif in Ezek 34*, 358. In Ezek 34 the lexeme *b^etôkem* (*among them*, v 24) is indeed epexegetic or explanatory of the import of the former one *'ălêhem* (*over them*, v 23).
19 Joshua was among the men sent out from the twelve tribes of Israel by Moses at Yahweh's command to go and spy out the land of Canaan (cf. Num 13:1–21). He was also among the few survivors in the wilderness (cf. Num 26:65) and was commissioned by Moses to lead the people into the Promised Land (cf. Num 27–15–23; Deut 1:38; 3:28). Interestingly this Hebrew name *Yehôshua'* (Joshua) "Yahweh is salvation" is the same name given to the saviour of the world. Joseph was asked to accept his mysteriously pregnant wife Mary: "She will bear a son, and you are to name him *Jesus, for he will save his people from their sins*" (Matt 1:21). The difference between the normal Jewish name *Joshua* and *Jesus* is that Jesus is the Christ (Greek, *Christos*) meaning the *Anointed One of God* or the *Messiah* (cf. John 1:41).

were standing near God. Therefore, both of them had the divine mandate to lead the people of God, and so Joshua was anointed unto service for the people (cf. Num 27:15–23). Like Moses, he was a focussed and spirit-filled leader. Deut 34:9 says: "And Joshua the son of Nun was full of the spirit of wisdom, for Moses had laid his hands upon him; so the people of Israel obeyed him, and did as the LORD had commanded Moses." He was interested not only in the material welfare of the people he was leading, but also in their spiritual well-being, since he knew that their having a good relationship with Yahweh, their God, would enhance their happiness on earth. He, therefore, led the people onto making a covenantal declaration at Shechem to worship Yahweh alone, so as to gain his blessings and avoid his anger (cf. Josh 24:14–28). In summary, Joshua can be called an ideal leader as this description of him shows:

> By his character, Joshua was stainless, humble and faithful to Moses, Yahweh and his people. As a citizen he was patriotic in the highest degree; as a warrior, he was fearless and blameless; as a judge, he was calm and impartial. He was quite equal to every emergency under which he was to act. He was valiant without temerity, active without precipitation. He did not neglect any lawful duty, care or advantage. His success was promoted by his ever obedience to divine direction with simplicity of mind.[20]

After the era of the great leaders like Moses and Joshua, the judges who were ad hoc charismatic leaders led the Israelites. They were chosen by Yahweh to liberate his people each time they were attacked by some enemies. The story of the judges runs like a refrain; Israel would do what was evil in the eyes of Yahweh; usually apostasy, by forsaking him and worshipping foreign gods. Yahweh would give them up to the powers of their enemies. After some time, they would cry to Yahweh for help and he would raise a leader, a judge, to rescue them from the shackles of the enemies. Among such leaders were Othniel (Judges 3:7–11), Ehud (3:12–30), Deborah (4:1–5:31), Gideon (6:1–8:32), Abimelech (8:30–9:57), Jephthah (10:6–12:7), Samson (13:1–16:31), and Samuel (1 Sam 7:2–17). For want of space; however, only three of them will be briefly examined here on account of the significance of their actions as leaders – Abimelech, Samson and Samuel.

---

20 G. O. Abe, "The Old Testament Concept of Leadership Role in Nation Building" in: *African Journal of Biblical Studies (AJBS)*, VI/1 (April, 1991) 32.

Abimelech: The name Abimelech (*'ăbîmelek*) literally means "my father is king," a name of a prince given to this person probably because he was a son of Gideon, who once led Israel as a judge. Abimelech was born to Gideon by his concubine who lived in Shechem, but Gideon had seventy other sons born by his numerous wives (cf. Judges 8:30–31). Following the narrative in Judges 9:1–21, Abimelech was an ambitious fellow and also very brutal and ready to shed much blood to grab a leadership position. When his father died, he evoked tribal sentiments in his maternal uncles by asking them to convince all the citizens of Shechem to support him to the throne by reminding them: "Remember also that I am your bone and your flesh". They said to themselves: "He is our brother", and so they obliged him and spoke on his behalf to the people of Shechem who then gave him their moral and financial support. To prevent any opposition, he went and hired some scoundrels who helped him in murdering the other seventy sons of Gideon, except one of them that was hidden at the time, Jotham (cf. Judges 9:2–6). He was made king by the people of Shechem and Beth-Millo, the leadership office that he got at the cost of the lives of other people. He was to them a brutal tyrant, and it did not take time before a spirit of discord came between him and the people of Shechem who supported him to the throne (cf. Judges 9:22–24). His shameful end was that in a battle, a woman threw a millstone at his head from a wall and he begged his armour-bearer to pierce him through with a sword, so that he died. His leadership is representative of any tyrannical and bloodthirsty dictator in the world.

Samson: The etymology of the personal name Samson (Heb. *Shimshôn*) is uncertain, and might perhaps have connection with the Hebrew word *shemesh* (sun) and a deity's name *Shamash*.[21] The birth of Samson was foretold by an angel of God who brought the good news of eventual child-bearing to a childless couple living in Zorah – Manoah and his wife. They were told that the child to be born would be a nazirite. He would never be given a haircut, and he would rescue Israel from the hands of the Philistines who were molesting them at the time (cf. Judges 13:1–5). The child later grew up and started fulfilling his destiny with special divine strength (cf.

---

21 See "Samson" in: John L. McKenzie, *Dictionary of the Bible* (London: Geoffrey Chapman, 1978) 767.

Judges 15:1–20). He got into a love relationship with a Philistine girl named Delilah. This woman eventually became his betrayer and a serious distraction of his destined duty. The Philistines paid her to ascertain from Samson the source of his unnatural strength. After a long trial, she succeeded in learning from him that, if he was shaved, he would become of normal strength. His hair was eventually shaved and he was so weakened that the Philistines tied him up, tortured him, and plucked out his eyes. At his prayer God gave him back some hair and strength with which he pulled down the temple of the Philistine god, Dagon, killing himself and the Philistines who mocked him in front of their god (cf. Judges 16:4–31). Samson represents the leaders who allow sensual things and material pursuits to distract them from performing their duties towards God and the people of God placed under their charge.

The Institution of the Monarchy: The last of the judges was Samuel.[22] He initially served in the shrine of Yahweh at Shiloh under the priest Eli (cf. 1 Sam 2:18–21), but later he became the people's judge or leader as 1 Sam 7:15 has noted: "Samuel was judge over Israel throughout his life." It was towards the end of his life that the monarchy was instituted in Israel, when he anointed Saul as the first King of Israel (cf. 1 Sam 10:1–27). Saul was eaten up by jealousy against his servant David after David's defeat of Goliath (cf. 1 Sam 17:1–54) and he kept seeking his life until he died (cf. 1 Sam 18:6–31:4). Saul was later succeeded by King David who was succeeded by his son Solomon, and so on. The Israelite kings will not be

---

22 The etymology of this name is a bit problematic. 1 Samuel 1:20 states: "In due time, Hannah conceived and bore a son. She named him Samuel, for she said, 'I have asked him of the LORD.'" This text purports that the name has to do with the verb of *asking*. Thus the note on the verse in the *New Jerusalem Bible* states: "A derivation from the root *sha'al* (to ask) would give *sha'ul* 'Saul.' Biblical etymology is often, as here, content with a certain similarity of sound. The actual derivation of 'Samuel' is from Shem-El, 'the name of God' or '(God's) name is El.'" However, I submit that judging from the circumstances of Samuel's birth; the barrenness of his mother Hannah, her prayer for a child, the prayerful assurance by the priest Eli that God would hear and grant her request, and the fulfillment of it in the child's birth (cf. 1 Sam 1:1–28), one can also think of the verb of hearing (*shāmaʿ*), and so *Samuel* could be an apocopate form of *shāmaʿ-El* which would mean "*God has heard*" my prayer.

treated individually here, since they are very many, rather reference will be made of some of them, when and where necessary.

When one looks closely at the OT's kingship or the Israelite monarchy, one would notice that almost all the narrations about their kings bear the judgemental statement that this or that king did what was pleasing or what was displeasing in the eyes of the Lord Yahweh (cf. for instance, 1 Kings 14:7–16; 2 Kings 10:31 and 2 Ch 33:1–2). Only a few of the kings were not indicted for doing what displeased Yahweh. Thus, in Sirach 49:4, we read: "Except David and Hezekiah and Josiah they all sinned greatly, for they forsook the law of the Most High...." Interestingly, David is here numbered among the "good kings" despite the two documented major faults of his, namely; his sins of adultery and murder against Uriah (cf. 2 Sam 11:1–12:10), and the controversial census he made which claimed the lives of thousands of Israelites (cf. 1 Ch 21:1–17). Reference is; however, made to his first fault: "David did what was right in the sight of the LORD, and did not turn aside from anything that he commanded him all the days of his life, except in the matter of Uriah the Hittite (1 Kings 15:5)." An important point is that the biblical evaluation of OT kings is very often based on how far they ruled in line with the Israelite covenantal law (the *Tôrāh*). They brought either a blessing or curse on themselves and on their people depending on how far they valued and acted on God's ordinances or the *law* (*Tôrāh*). As Edwin R. Thiele puts it, "The Hebrews were God's people.... Rulers were blessed to the degree that they continued being faithful to God, or cursed to the degree that they departed from the distinctive features of religious faith and practice."[23] The leaders who directly encouraged religious syncretism, or those who one way or another allowed the worship of idols, are usually described as misleaders. It is, for instance, said of King Manasseh (687–642 BC): "Manasseh misled Judah and the inhabitants of Jerusalem, so that they did more evil than the nations whom the LORD had destroyed before the people of Israel (2 Ch 33:9, NRS)." This is because he acted as a direct opposite of his father Hezekiah by fully encouraging idolatrous practices in Israel (cf. 2 Ch 33:1–8). He also committed other evils as John L. Mckenzie notes: "The record of Manasseh (2 K 21:1–17)

---

23 Edwin R. Thiele, *The Mysterious Numbers of the Hebrew Kings*, New Revised Edition (Grand Rapids: Kregel Publications, 1994) 193–194.

is the blackest of all the kings of Judah, he is credited with the worship of foreign gods, superstition of all kinds, oppression and murder, and becomes the occasion of the decision of Yahweh to destroy Judah."[24] Conversely, King Josiah is said to have destroyed the altars of the idols in Israel and so restored the true worship of Yahweh during his own time (cf. 2 Kings 23:19–24). He is rated among their best leaders from the point of view of acting in line with the *law*. In 2 Ch 34:33 (NIV), we read: "Josiah removed all the detestable idols from all the territory belonging to the Israelites, and he had all who were present in Israel serve the LORD their God. As long as he lived, they did not fail to follow the LORD, the God of their fathers."

It would be an overstretch to posit that the observance of the *law* as the only acid test for good or bad leadership in Israel. Their leaders were equally expected to show care and concern towards the people placed under their care by Yahweh. Thus, the Prophet Ezekiel was commanded by Yahweh to pronounce a serious oracle of indictment *against the shepherds of Israel* (*'al-rô'ê yisrā'ēl*, i.e., their leaders), because of their failure to care for their flock (their people), but they were rather exploiting them. So, he says:

> The word of the LORD came to me: "Son of man, prophesy against the shepherds of Israel, prophesy, and say to them, even to the shepherds, Thus says the Lord GOD: Ho, shepherds of Israel who have been feeding yourselves! Should not shepherds feed the sheep? You eat the fat, you clothe yourselves with the wool, you slaughter the fatlings; but you do not feed the sheep. The weak you have not strengthened, the sick you have not healed, the crippled you have not bound up, the strayed you have not brought back, the lost you have not sought, and with force and harshness you have ruled them (cf. Ezek 34:1–4, RSV)."

The indicted shepherds (leaders) were only interested in what they could get from the sheep (people), without thinking of what they could do to enhance their well-being. The oracle tends to show that Israel had had some experiences of leaders who exhibited highhanded and unbecoming behaviours. For instance, King Rehoboam, the son of King Solomon, was asked by his people to lighten the burden of the forced labour which his father had laid on them. His attitude to the people's plea was very harsh. He said that he would increase rather than reduce the burden, a clear sign that he intended to be autocratic in his type of leadership. The reaction of

---

24 See "Manasseh" in: John L. McKenzie, *Dictionary of the Bible*, 540.

the people to that response was that of rejection, and it led to the splitting of Israel into two antagonistic zones; the Northern and the Southern Kingdoms (cf. 1 Kings 12:1–19). One can equally remember here the story of King Ahab and one of his subjects, Naboth the Jezreelite; the king asked for a piece of land belonging to Naboth but it was not given to him, so he allowed his wife Jezebel to get Naboth murdered, after which he took over the land (cf. 1 Kings 21:1–19). There were also leaders who murdered anybody regarded by them as an opponent. For instance, Queen Athaliah murdered all possible heirs to the throne, just to create space for her to rule (cf. 2 Ch 22:10–12). However, the same oracle presents Yahweh as the Good Shepherd who demonstrates through his provident and caring attitude what an *ideal shepherd or leader* should look like; exactly what the negligent shepherds/leaders were expected to do but they failed, that is what he promised to do for the flock (cf. Ezek 34:11–16).[25]

There were also good leaders, even non-Israelite ones, who thought of the welfare of those under their care. For instance, when King Cyrus[26] of Persia conquered Babylon, he considered the convenience of all the people conquered by King Nebuchadnezzar of Babylon and allowed them to return to their homes. Of him Yahweh says through the prophet Isaiah: "'He is my shepherd, and he shall carry out all my purpose'; and who says of Jerusalem, 'It shall be rebuilt,' and of the temple, 'Your foundation shall be laid' (Isa 44:28)." McKenzie notes that "This hope was fulfilled in 538 BC when Cyrus permitted the Jews residing in Babylon to return to Jerusalem and rebuild the city and its temple (2 Ch 36:22f; Ezr 1:1–4)."[27] In résumé, one can say that living according to the *Law* (*Tôrāh*) is presented as the fundamental leadership guide in the OT just as living according to the *law*

---

25 For discussion on the bad and good leadership styles (Ezek 34:1–10, 11–16), see Ignatius M.C. Obinwa, *"I Shall Feed Them with Good Pasture" (Ezek 34:14). The Shepherd Motif in Ezek 34: Its Theological Import and Socio-political Implications*, FzB 125 (Würzburg: Echter Verlag, 2012) 273–337.

26 The name Cyrus is given in Hebrew as *Kôresh* (cf. Isa 45:1) and in Persian language as *Kurash*, meaning 'shepherd.' He acted as a good shepherd towards his vassals, including the Jews whom he released from their Babylonian bondage.

27 See "Cyrus" in: John L. McKenzie, *Dictionary of the Bible*, 167.

of love and service is that of the NT.[28] But the case of the non-Jewish leader Cyrus mentioned above shows that the *Law* (*Tôrāh*) is not a *sine-qua-non*, rather it is the leader showing care and consideration for the well-being of the led that counts for good leadership in the OT and everywhere.

5. Leadership in the African Context

Generally in African communities, leadership rests in the hands of a group of elderly persons known as the council of elders (gerontocracy). There are relatively very few cases of absolute monarchy where a single individual wields power alone. According to E. E. Uzukwu, "There are, first of all, societies with dispersal of authority or with authority in the hands of many… Then there are those societies with centralized authority… The idea of the exercise of authority by many leaders … appears to be the most common pattern of social organization in sub-Saharan Africa".[29] It is in those places where a kingship or monarchy is hereditary that centralised authority is generally found; such as, in Ganda. Centralised authority is sometimes found also in those places where leadership office is elective, as in Oyo, Nigeria. As Uzukwu notes further, in few places like Mali and Songhai, the centralised authority tends towards being autocratic or dictatorial: "This was the prevalent situation in those kingdoms; such as, Mali and Songhai, which were under the influence of Arab-Moslem culture. The rulers (Mansa or Askia as they were called) appointed military commanders or slaves over provinces and districts, and these were directly responsible to the rulers. This kind of dictatorship is not characteristic of typical African kingdoms…."[30] Usually an African monarchy is oligarchic in nature; there is some sharing of leadership authority between the king and the other chiefs

---

28 To teach his disciples what good leadership should be like Jesus says to them: "You know that among the Gentiles those whom they recognise as their rulers lord it over them, and their great ones are tyrants over them. But it is not so among you; but whoever wishes to become great among you must be your servant, and whoever wishes to be first among you must be slave of all. For the Son of Man came not to be served but to serve, and to give his life a ransom for many" (Mark 10:42–45).

29 Elochukwu E. Uzukwu, *A Listening Church: Autonomy and Communion in African Churches* (Maryknoll: Orbis Books, 1996) 14.

30 Uzukwu, *A Listening Church*, 16.

representing the various arms of the large society. "The monarchies which
are oligarchic are the more typical African pattern of kingship. There is a
monarch, but the exercise of authority is collegial...the Bini, Oyo, Egba,
Hausa, Ashanti, Abomey, Zulu, Kongo, Swazi, and Ganda kingdoms are
examples of such oligarchic monarchies (though the Hausa kingdoms were
later influenced by Islamic culture after the Dan Fodio jihad and became
centralized and autocratic." [31]

In traditional African communities, the democratic leadership style is
more common. In this leadership style, dictatorship is circumvented through
enabling the common people to express their views directly or through their
representatives and thus authority is placed in the hands of many. This is
commonly found among small communities like the pygmies of Central
Africa, the San of the Kalahari Desert, and among some large communities like the Igbo people[32] of Nigeria. Uzukwu adds: "This preference for
the exercise of authority by many is also realized in fairly populous ethnic
groups which are not receptive to a strong and centralized authority. An
interesting example is the Igbo of Nigeria, who would be counted in the millions during the period under review." [33] One can then use the Igbo people
as an example of the many African democratic communities.

The type of leadership found in Igbo-land can be described as gerontocracy, which involves various families being represented by their eldest
male members, since the elderly females must have been married before
they become of age. The exercise of leadership begins from the nuclear
and reaches the extended families. The eldest father of a nuclear family is
known as *Okpala* (i.e., firstborn) and plays the leadership role within the
nuclear family (called *ezinuno*). In the traditional setting, he holds the family *Ofo* (*a sacred stick symbolic of justice and righteousness*). As the family
extends through children marrying and begetting children, who later marry
and beget grand children, etc., there exist then many *Okpalas* (firstborns)

---

31 Uzukwu, *A Listening Church*, 16–17.
32 The Igbo people live in the south eastern part of Nigeria. They number about
   forty million people. Cf. http://en.wikipedia.org/wiki/Igbo_people, accessed on
   20.05.2014.
33 Uzukwu, *A Listening Church*, 14–15. See also Francis Anekwe Oborji, *Trends
   in African Theology since Vatican II. A Missiological Orientation* (Roma: Tipo-
   grafica Leberit, 1998) 16–17.

or holders of *Ofo* (*nde ji Ofo* or *ndi oji Ofo*) within the extended family or kindred (known as *Umunna*). These holders of *Ofo* would then form the council of elders who oversee the socio-political well-being of the village. When they assemble together for a community discussion, the *Okpala* of the mother-family (known as *Obi*) presides, because he holds the *Ofo Umunna*, but he does so as a *primus inter pares,* because he is not allowed to dictate or veto on issues concerning the rest. Issues are discussed and the views of the various family representatives are given due consideration. It is when a consensus is reached that the presiding Okpala (*Obi*) would stamp it with the *Ofo Umunna* that he is holding. The same process continues from the kindred level (*Umunna*) to the village level (*Ogbe* with *Ofo Ogbe*), and from there to the town level (*Obodo* with *Ofo Obodo*). Thus in the words of Onyema Anozie,

> In Igbo community, the government of the people rests on the *Ofo* holders at the town level. Traditionally African towns are made up of villages, who come together to make up the town… at the town level the *oji Ofo* gather to form what could be referred to as the governing council, literally regarded as "*Ndi oji Ofo*" – holders of *Ofo*. This is the highest governing arm in the town. Matters of town interest or matters which could not be resolved at the village level are brought to the *oji Ofo* who look into it and give their verdict.[34]

It is a listening type of leadership that is practised in traditional Igbo societies, because the family's elders who represent their various nuclear families go to meetings of their extended families with the views of their nuclear family members. Then, those that go to the meetings of the villages and the towns do so, bearing the opinions of the members of their extended families. The traditional Igbo leaders can be described as good listeners since they do not behave like dictators who, as bad leaders that they are, do not pay attention to the views and complaints of the people placed under their charge. Since the Igbo people are used as a sample, it is clear that such a listening style of leadership is widespread in other traditional African societies. Uzukwu says:

---

34 Onyema Anozie, "A Moral Evaluation of the Igbo Concept of Leadership in a Multi-ethno Community" in: Ferdinand Nwaigbo, *et al* (eds.), *Ethnicity and Christian Leadership in West African Sub-Region* (Port Harcourt: CIWA Publications, 2004) 193.

Among the Manja of the Central African Republic the totem for the chief is the
rabbit because this unobtrusive animal has "large ears". As is common all over Africa, the chief is considered to be very close to God, the ancestors and the protective
spirits of the community.... The Manja underline "listening" as the most dominant
characteristic of the chief. His "large ears" bring him close to God, ancestors and
divinities, and close to the conversations taking place in the community. He has
the "last word". This is because he speaks after having assimilated and digested
the word of the community.[35]

The idea mentioned above that among the Israelites the people's leaders are
regarded as representing God among his people is equally found among the
African people. John S. Mbiti says about African traditional rulers: "These
rulers are symbolically the representatives of God on earth, and sometimes
the same terms are used of both them and God. Just as God is the king,
ruler and governor of the universe, so these human rulers are the kings,
rulers and governors of their particular people. They exercise an authority
believed to come from God.... Some of these rulers are also the chief priests,
acting as the religious links between their people and God. In ruling they are
performing not only political duties, but also religious duties."[36] The same
idea is embedded in the title *Igwe* (chief) which is given by the Igbo people
to the leader of a town (*Obodo*). The term *Igwe* literally means *heaven*
and its figurative semantic import is *God* (who dwells in *heaven*). An *Igwe*
is the *Obi* or *Okpala* of the oldest family in the town who holds the *Ofo
Obodo*. Another name for such a town leader in some Igbo communities
is *Eze* (literally, *king*), a title which is also applicable to God as the King of
the universe (*Eze-uwa*). It is noteworthy; however, that despite such honour-
able and quasi divine titles (*Igwe* and *Eze*), the Igbo town leaders are not
deified nor do they arrogate divine powers to themselves. They do not even
dictate to their people, because the other *Okpalas* who form the council
of elders are the coadjutors of the *Igwe/Eze* and their opinions cannot be
simply ignored, since autocracy is not tolerated in Igbo-land. The Igbo form
of democracy is of a high quality, and the consideration of people's views is

---

35 Elochukwu E. Uzukwu, "A Servant Church in a New African Nation: Leader-
    ship as a Service of Listening," *Bulletin of Ecumenical Theology*, vol. 6/1: 1994,
    23. See also Uzukwu, *A Listening Church*, 127.
36 John S. Mbiti, *Introduction to African Religion* (NY: Praeger Publishers, 1975)
    162.

such that some neighbours see it as overstretched and clumsy, and so they say that *Igbo people have no king* (*Igbo enwe eze*). Positively considered, it really means that autocracy or dictatorship is not tolerated within the Igbo's leadership system. As Uzukwu remarks, among the Igbo people, "Orders which come from the top without prior discussion or negotiation are ignored."[37] This democratic style of leadership practised in Igbo-land and the afore-mentioned oligarchic monarchies in some parts of Africa present the real picture of the traditional leadership system in Africa. The few autocratic cases mentioned above are due to an external influence; such as, the Arab-Moslem incursion that made some African leaders lose their traditional African democratic system of leadership.

6. Conclusion

Our discussion above shows that there is some similarity between the Old Testament's concept of leadership and the African one. In both there are individual cases of those who lead the people with humane consideration and those who are highhanded and exploitative of those they led. It is interesting that both of them hold that human leaders are simply representatives of God, because the whole world and its entire people belong to God – Jews and non-Jews alike (cf. Ps 24:1). The implication is that the people being led *belong* to God and not to the leaders as their slaves. Therefore, the leaders of any people in the world are answerable to God with regard to the way they treat those placed under their care. This demands that all those who rise to the position of leadership must act according to the mind of God. Good leadership would then involve the realisation that being at the helm of affairs or occupying the position of authority demands working hard to provide advantages to the people being led rather than taking advantage of them or exploiting them. Recapitulating our definitions, good leadership would involve setting reachable goals that would be advantageous to the whole community, searching for the best means of realising the goals, initiating ideas and projects that would serve the common good of all, and working together with the whole community, especially with the experts towards achieving the set goals. With regard to the leadership

---

37 Uzukwu, *A Listening Church*, 15.

styles, we saw that the OT's narrators have quite honestly presented us with both the good and the bad types of leaders. For instance, the good or considerate ones like Moses (Exod 3:1ff) and even the foreign King Cyrus of Persia (cf. 2 Ch 36:22–23) are worthy of emulation. It is clear that the wicked and exploitative type of leadership shown by such OT leaders as King Abimelech who murdered 69 people to clear his way to the throne (cf. Judges 9:2–6), King Ahab who murdered his subject Naboth in order to take his land (cf. 1 Kings 21:1–16), Saul who kept thirsting for the blood of his servant David out of jealousy (cf. 1 Sam 18:6–31:4), or even some acts of David himself who planned the death of his subject Uriah just to cover his sin of adultery with Uriah's wife and to save his face from shame (2 Sam 11:1–17), are not recommended. On the contrary, it is easy to see how recommendable the African/Igbo style of democracy is, because it excludes dictatorship by being people-involving, and has very good "listening ears" without degenerating to a *laissez-faire* type of leadership.[38] The fact that there have been and there are good leaders both in the Israelite nation and in African nations shows that it is possible to be a just and righteous leader, if only the individual wants to. Thus, as Nwachukwu has noted, "God's authority is represented on earth through the Church. So, through her social organization and leadership, the Church bears witness that a redemptive use of power is possible within the human community."[39] If only those who rise to the leadership positions would put it before their memory that they are there to serve God among his people, they would do well and be remembered as good leaders. It must be said with a sense of joy that indeed many State Governors in Nigeria, as well as other people in leadership positions are measuring up positively to their demands of their offices and showing that it is possible to really be a good leader. In the prologue to his famous Code, the ancient Babylonian King Hammurabi (1800 B.C.) demonstrates

---

38 However, the Jesus' leadership-model which entails zero exploitation and the readiness to serve or to take trouble for the good of others rather than the eagerness to be served by them (cf. Mark 10:42–45), remains the most recommendable leadership style ever. Paul emphasises one aspect of the Jesus' model of leadership by proposing the transparency or honesty model; meaning that leaders should be worthy of emulation (cf. 1 Tim 4:12).

39 MarySylvia Nwachukwu, "Biblical Framework for a Spirituality of Collaborative Ministry" in: Ignatius M.C. Obinwa (ed.), *Collaborative Ministry*. 66.

this of his awareness serving his gods through the righteous fulfilment of his duties towards the people by saying:

> When lofty Anum, king of the Anunnaki,
> (and) Enlil, lord of heaven and earth,
> the determiner of the destinies of the land,
> determined for Marduk, the first-born of Enki...
> **at that time Anum and Enlil named me**
> **to promote the welfare of the people,**
> **me, Hammurabi, the devout, god-fearing prince,**
> **to cause justice to prevail in the land,**
> **to destroy the wicked and the evil,**
> **that the strong might not oppress the weak,**
> to rise like the sun over the black-headed (people),
> and to light up the land.
> Hammurabi, the shepherd, called by Enlil, am I;
> **the one who makes affluence and plenty abound;**
> **who provides in abundance all sorts of things** for Nippur-Duranki....[40] (*I added the emphasis for clarity*).

Therefore, King Hammurabi regarded his leadership role as that of divinely assigned service towards the people placed under his care by their gods. "His duties included the provision of social amenities, causing justice to prevail in the land, putting an end to wickedness by keeping evil people in check, so that the strong might not oppress the weak. He was therefore concerned about the general welfare of his people."[41] All contemporary leaders should take note, because their case is not different vis-à-vis the God who owns the whole universe.

---

40 James B. Pritchard (ed.), *ANET*, p. 164. See also Daniel I. Block, *The Book of Ezekiel*, pp. 280–281.

41 Ignatius M. C. Obinwa, *"I Shall Feed Them with Good Pasture" (Ezek 34:14). The Shepherd Motif in Ezekiel 34: Its Theological Import and Socio-political Implications*, Forschung zur Bibel 125 (Würzburg: Echter Verlag, 2012), p. 220.

Augustine C. O. Oburota

Reforming Seminary Formation for Effective Pastoral and Spiritual Leadership

1. Introduction

The Church is said to be in continuous reformation – *ecclesia semper refor-manda*. This phrase is associated with Karl Barth, Calvin, and the Reformed Church, although it was much earlier used by St. Augustine. As is evident in Church history, the seminary too gets reformed along with the Church, perhaps because the role of priests is quite essential to spiritual progress in the life of the Church. Indeed, right from the time of our Lord Jesus Christ, seminary reforms have been ongoing. The Vatican II word for the need to effect changes according to the demands of the times is *Aggiornamento*, bringing up to date.

Seminary formation has always had a central and permanent question: how can future priests be trained so that they become other Christ(s) to the world? This tends to be the basic question also in Christian life in general, formation for imitating Christ. Every discussion about what we do and what others expect of Christians is always that – are we/you like Christ? A lot of ink has been spilled in comments about Mahatma Ghandi's alleged historic statement: "I like your Christ, I do not like your Christians. Your Christians are so unlike your Christ." This is like, "where is the Christ in your Christians?" St. Paul would say, "for me to live is Christ and to die is gain" (Phil.1:21). Many would agree that to talk of a good priest is to talk of a priest who is a good Christ; the same applies when one is talking about a good Christian. A non-German would find it very interesting to notice that the German word for a Christian is "Christ" ("Christen" pl.). Christ is always good, and this leaves the clergy and the laity with no alternative. Indeed, with regard to the priesthood, the problem has always been that some priests live their priesthood as if there is an alternative to living it as Christ. It's all about living out the virtues of Christ's own priesthood like: power of faith, holiness, humility, service to God, self-sacrifice for others" salvation, love or christian charity, and generosity. When we talk of reform in seminary formation, it is all about better forms of seminary training, in so far as what is new that can make priests like Christ and be able to address the present challenges in evangelisation.

Priesthood training is successful only when it turns out future priests who are entirely dedicated to God and passionate about uplifting people spiritually. How can this be achieved? Do our seminaries need reform? Both are necessary. On one hand, there is the priest whose lifestyle is in itself deeply spiritual with a deep relationship with God. On the other hand, there is the priest whose presence is always a force that draws people closer to God. As someone once involved in formation as a formator, these two issues have bothered me: how does one form these candidates to be strong enough in their spiritual life and for their entire life bring people nearer to God. The life of the priest seems to hinge on those two relationship challenges.

The terms in our essay are: "reform," "seminary," "formation," "effective," "pastoral," "spiritual," and "leadership." We will define them in the course of this essay. Our ultimate concern is the possibility of discovering a compelling method of forming future priests who would be forever faithful, in other words, *semper fidelis* priests.

2. Reforming of Seminaries for Leadership – Short History

The following is a history of antecedents in seminary reform, and much of our information here comes from John Tracy Ellis" *Essays in Seminary Education*, 1967.

It all begins with Jesus Christ and his disciples, and the selection of the apostles – the first seminary. The pattern of priestly training during the early or post-resurrection Church period may have remained the same as the "first seminary," the disciples "being with" Jesus, and learning from him about how to be apostles. During the period immediately after this "first seminary," there were already appointments of deacons, priests, and bishops. We read in the *Didache* (late 1st century) about the priestly service: "… For they, too (bishops and deacons), render you the sacred service of the prophets and teachers." St. Polycarp (d. AD 155), writes: "The presbyter must be tender-hearted, merciful toward all, turning back the sheep that has gone astray, visiting the sick, not neglecting the widow or orphan or poor man..." This enumerates the qualities and work of a good priest. In the letter to the Hebrews, we have a description of the priesthood of Christ and in the New Testament, it states what a model priest should be after the example of Christ.

The next is the patristic period. It is known that during this period in the Church the get-together in one place remained the same as in the very early Church. The bishop had a close eye on seminarians. Community, or "being with," was still emphasised. The weakness of clerical formation in the modern age will be blamed on a certain distancing between formation and community, between seminary and bishop. It would not be right if it was all about learning and only learning. The spiritual, social, and intellectual training should take place together. St. Augustine is known to have showed concern about the importance of community in the training.

In his time, St. Benedict (480–547), one of the fathers of western monasticism, would design a special training program for candidates of a monastic life. "Ora et labora" was his motto. There would be time for manual labour, sacred reading, and prayers. Of course, leisure times were provided. By the time of Bede (672–735), the three forms of studies, the *trivium*, had evolved and were very much in use in the Church. According to St. Bede: "I have spent all the remainder of my life in this monastery and devoted myself entirely to the study of the Scriptures. And while I have observed the regular discipline and sung the choir offices daily in Church, my chief delight has always been in study, teaching, and writing." Studies during this period had the form of the *trivium*: reading, writing, and speaking. The early medieval period from the time of Boethius (480–524) would later introduce the *quadrivium*: arithmetic, geometry, astronomy, and music. Future priests would begin to undergo these studies.

The Middle Ages in western history spanned between the fifth and the fifteenth centuries. This period would see the monastic model of schooling throughout the western world. Not only monasteries, but also schools would preoccupy the Church's attention. An example was the monastery of Fulda founded by St. Boniface. Emperor Charlemagne in the eighth century would decree that all clerics learn to read and write. They were to acquire knowledge to fulfil teaching duties. Lack of this knowledge meant suspension and a loss of office. Cathedral schools were as important as monastic schools and both played important roles in the training of priests. All this would lead to the opening of universities for higher studies.

St. Leander presided at the Fourth Council of Toledo in 633. He is known to have pushed for the promulgation of a law making it obligatory for priesthood candidates to come together in a single building at the cathedral premises. The environment was considered necessary to help the seminarians do pastoral work while in training and also to think more pastorally – integral formation.

Problems would be noticed in priestly training towards the end of the Middle Ages. Laxity would be noticed in clerical life. Pope Adrian VI in 1522 is known to have taken some actions. It would be noticed that the lack of institutions specifically for priestly formation was a major and costly omission. The monastic schools were not enough. The Council of Trent would intervene and address in a comprehensive manner aspects of formation and education of the clergy. According to Antonio Cardinal del Monte: "The aim of the reforming activity is the revival of the pastoral ministry–the cure of souls."

Pope Paul III was pope of clerical reform in the Church. He constituted a commission in 1536 for this purpose. The commission submitted a report to the Pope in 1537. It looked at the causes of weakness and clerical abuses. Furthermore, in 1547 clerical reform continued to be the major issue of discourse. Giovanni Cardinal Morone would suggest that the new Jesuit order open a college in Rome. He also suggested that German candidates for the priesthood be sent there. The Pope, Julius III, would welcome that. In February 1551, the college was opened. By 1565 nearly one thousand students attended lectures in philosophy and theology.

Reginald Cardinal Pole would in November of 1555 decree as follows: "that in cathedrals there be educated a certain number of beginners, from which, as from a seed bed (*seminarium*), priests can be chosen who can worthily be placed in charge of churches." We see here how the word "seminary" would originate – school for training of priests. The Latin "seminarium" is literally a "seed plot" and this meaning would be transferred to formation as a period of nursery. The decree by Reginald Cardinal Pole would reflect in the Council of Trent. Trent's decree regarding seminaries in 1563 would state as follows (we summarise):

- Cathedral and metropolitan Churches are to have a seminaries of their own.
- Smaller and poorer jurisdictions can jointly own what today we call a regional seminary.
- Every diocese is obliged to have a seminary, though not every candidate whom a bishop ordains has to be educated in a seminary.
- Candidates for the seminary are to be at least twelve years of age with skills in reading and writing and shall be of suitable moral character.
- The sons of the poor are to be given preference.
- Intellectual formation is to be according to a candidate's age and abilities.
- A normal curriculum of formation is to specify the following: study of the letters, the humanities, chant, and the science of "ecclesiastical computation," scripture, dogmatic, moral and pastoral theology, and rubrics.
- Part of spiritual formation is wearing the clerical dress, receiving the tonsure, daily Mass, going to Confession once a month, and to Holy Communion according to the direction of one's spiritual director.
- Seminary professors are to be qualified academically as follows: master's, licentiate, or doctoral degrees in the particular field of their expertise. They are to be competent in all their responsibilities.

Other details would then follow. The above would serve as both the uniform standard for the training of priests and the basis for weeding out unsuitable candidates. It can be clearly seen that reform is ongoing. Reform here can be defined as a change or an amendment for the purpose of improvement on what has been.

St. Ignatius, founder of the Society of Jesus, Jesuits, was a chief reformer of seminaries. Indeed, it became the turn of those responsible to carry on the reform of the Council of Trent. The following also worked hard in the standardisation of seminary training: Sulpicians (founded by Jean-Jacques Olier), the Vincentians, the Eudists (Congregation of Jesus and Mary), the Dominicans, the Carmelites, and the Franciscans. The following areas would be strengthened: academic curriculum, the spiritual life, discipline, and prayer life. Other areas are finance and administration. They were preoccupied with better results. When we talk of effectiveness, we refer to the desired results, and it is easy to see that the various reforms are indeed passionate about the foreseeable positive results.

St. Charles Cardinal Borromeo, the metropolitan of Milan, made some unforgettable contributions, although many of them were influences of Ignatius' *Spiritual Exercises*. He would influence other (seminary) reformers like Jean-Jacques Olier and St. Vincent de Paul. At Eichstätt in 1564, the first German seminary would be opened. Douai College in England would be established in 1568 for English and Irish dioceses. In France, the following were also known for clerical reforms: Adrien Bourdoise and Cardinal Pierre de Bérulle. Bourdoise opened a formation house at St. Nicholas de Chardonnet in 1612. Bérulle founded the French Oratory in 1611. He also saw to the opening of two other seminaries in Paris (1612) and Langres (1616). France's post-Tridentine influence in seminary formation is known to have been universal and up to the present day. Among others, the Sulpicians would continue to do a lot to raise the level of academics.

From time to time, governments have been involved in what concerns the seminary. Emperor Joseph and Leopold of the Holy Roman Empire in 1780–1790 suspended diocesan seminaries and approved of only state seminaries. In Bismarck's *Kulturkampf* candidates for the priesthood are to spend three years at a state university and take a state examination before qualifying as priests. That is how the dual system of seminary education, for example in Belgium, would come about. Seminaries would be built close to or right in universities.

The national seminary of St. Patrick's at Maynooth was opened in 1794 and All Hallows College in Dublin in 1842. They originated as a result of the debate on whether seminarians and lay students should study together. These two institutions were meant only for seminarians.

With its torture of priests and bishops, the French Revolution (1789–1799) would be responsible for priests leaving France to other countries like England, the US, and Canada.

In the 18th century, the Sulpicians sent some priests to America. They would begin a new seminary, St. Mary's Seminary, known to be the first seminary in the US. The religious and the secular clergy would subsequently open seminaries. The patristic method of a bishop training future priests by himself, though with the help of some priests, would be reintroduced by some priests. Seminaries would also spring up that served particularly the needs of ethnic groups, like the Irish, German, and Polish Americans. In 1857, the North American College would begin in Rome. Then in 1889, the Catholic University of America would be opened with money donated by a laywoman, although at this time it was only a theological institute for priests.

Discussion on the state of the seminaries would not cease to resurface, this time, at the third council of Baltimore (1884). Directives would be issued for better education in English and Greek. Other issues raised were: a need for vacation for seminarians, seminary formators, and teachers; as well as the need for apologetics with regard to some courses. James Cardinal Gibbons (1834–1921) made a critique of the seminary during his time in *The Ambassador of Christ*. He would call for formation in broadmindedness, as well as in solid intellectual formation. Fr. John Talbot Smith also in his "Our Seminaries: An essay on Clerical Training'" (1896) made relevant contributions. Fr. John Hogan would call for ongoing formation of priests, believing that even after ordination all aspects of priestly formation can still be furthered and deepened. We can see here the birth of the discussion ongoing formation of priests. Formation can be defined as a process of shaping in training. There is no doubt that if priests would become good spiritual and pastoral leaders, the seminary must undertake that.

At the beginning of the twentieth century, it would be clear that in the academic sphere not much remarkable would be noticed among priests. Academics did not seem to have attained the expected heights. Causes were identified as: academics in the seminary were not creative enough – just being assimilated for exams' sake; dioceses did not promote intellectualism; and religious superiors thought of intellectual exploits as dangerous to priestly life. Some would interpret the encyclical of St. Pius X, *Pascendi dominici gregis* (1907) as militating against academics of clerics.

The Vatican II (1962–65) would be known for famous documents that would never cease to influence discussions on formation of priests. Think of the following documents on the Church *Lumen gentium*, on the priesthood *Presbyterorum ordinis* and on seminary formation *Optatam totius*. In 1967, Blessed Pope Paul VI gave the world his encyclical on celibacy *Sacerdotalis caelibatus*. All these would influence conferences of Catholic bishops all over the world. Directives upon directives would be produced, especially for local seminaries. The Congregation for Clergy and the Congregation for Catholic Education also came up with several documents on different topics: patristics, philosophy, canon law, homiletics, as well as on spiritual and liturgical matters. We cannot overlook the great importance of several other documents, including the *Catechism of the Catholic Church* (promulgated 1992), and the *Code of Canon Law* (CIC, 1983). There is no doubt that an ongoing renewal has been going on all through the Church's history. As time went on, it no longer lasted decades and centuries before something was done. Since priesthood challenges are ongoing, efforts at seeking improvements and solutions should be done on a daily basis. Formators are also challenged on how to put all this into practice. The Vatican II is known to be a pastoral council and this has not ceased to make its impact in seminary formation; pastoral here being defined as related to "spiritual herdsmanship." The priest has to lead those he is responsible for as a visionary leader, focused on the goal.

Pope St. John Paul II began an annual address to priests each Holy Thursday. The 8th Ordinary Synod of Bishops held in 1990 had the theme, "The Formation of Priests in Circumstances of the Present Day." St. John Paul II would bring the fruits together in his post-synodal apostolic exhortation *Pastores dabo vobis* (*I Will Give You Shepherds*) in 1992. This document has been very influential owing to its comprehensiveness. With it, the question now may not be in content, but in bringing the content into practice during formation of priests. This Pope would be famous for his sustained concern for improvement in formation.

3. Counting the Blessings

One can rightly claim that the efforts of the Church at reforming seminary formation through the centuries have really paid off. Paradoxically, it is one of the things that the recent priest abuse scandals would show. The scandals were horrid, outrageous, and shameful indeed. What would make a priest so mean as to abuse the other person? What can be said about priests abusing minors? Debates and discussions are found in books, on the dailies, radio and television, on the internet, and at seminars and conferences. It can be said that nothing worse has ever happened to the Church in modern times. However, all these discussions have led to the examination of what is really going on, not only in the priesthood but also in society at large.

It is said that while priests' pedophilia in the US is put at 1.4% (or 2%), in the general population the rate is 4%, and easy access to little children is also blamed. Moreover, 79.9% of abusers are married, and this questions the credibility of the view that holds that it all has to do with celibacy and priests not being married. So, it would now be questionable to say, "If you don't want to be a pedophile go and marry." Surprisingly the reply comes, "The married are the worst pedophiles." Moreover, 60% of abuses are by parents, and 4–5% are by the children's teachers. Another alarming finding is that non-Catholic clergy are worse than the Catholics by 11%. So, part of the issue is that priests' abuse is far lower in percentage than of any other group.

Without being a real credit to the Church, knowing that one single abuse is one too many, it makes one ask why is it that priests are not as bad as others. This may likely be pointing at the relatively high standard of training for priests. It may be the fact that pastoral and spiritual leadership in the priesthood is relatively effective. By leadership here we mean establishing or sharing a clear vision from the head and taking others along to it. I have seen an interesting poster about a good and a bad leader. It shows a bad leader sitting high up and pointing the way to others without joining in the movement towards the goal. The good leader, on the contrary, points the way, comes down from his high position, and joins in the movement towards the goal. This depicts typical leadership in the Church. The priest leader is as serious in pleasing God as in helping his flock in reaching God. Yet, this does not necessarily answer the question of why a priest should be involved in abuse of any kind – pedophilia, ephebophilia (abuse of adults), homosexuality, and so forth. These offences show that some priests are leaders but not necessarily spiritual leaders. By "spiritual" we mean being religious and open to the otherworldly, not being materialistic or carnal.

What would make a priest, in spite of long period of nurture and quality formation, to let somebody down? Abuses are obviously antithetical to the teachings of Christ. What then would make a priest a pedophile? The following views were mainly gathered from internet articles. Some have pointed at some possible reasons why a priest would abuse his neighbour. Predator priests are said to be those who were not supposed to have been ordained at all; they went in there to exploit people. These may have got in unnoticed, just to enjoy the respect associated with the profession/vocation. Some priest abusers are said to be mental patients who were supposed to have been screened out with the help of psychological assessment during formation. Others hold that these perverted priests are simply evil people. Opinions are as varied as there are different ideologies and orientation. Mel Gibson, the maker of the film, The Passion of Christ, is known to have blamed the Vatican II for corrupting the Church and the priesthood. Others have also blamed the "male culture," as well as the declining morals of the 20th century.

4. Leadership

Leadership appears last in our list of important terms above, but it seems to be the key to understanding the aim of this essay. Leadership is known to connote the following: mastery, guidance, direction, authority, control, management, supervision, prosperity, mastery, initiative, influence, and organization. Does leadership really have to do with effectiveness as a priest and carer for souls? Yes, indeed, knowing that the Church is a body, comprising various groups and communities. Leadership must have to do with it. Dwight D. Eisenhower on leadership is known for saying that, "Leadership is the art of getting someone else to do something you want done because he wants it." This view of leadership, oft quoted, would really show what Christian leadership is all about, as well as how necessary it can be in the priesthood. True leaders are known for vision or the pursuit of some end and leading others to it. They are known for their passion for creating something new as a result of their focus and docility. For us Christians, the sole end or goal in our endeavours is Christ or the kingdom of heaven, and this is always borne in mind in all we do. The followers expect that the leader cuts the path for the rest and he or she directs others on the right way until they get there. They also expect that he or she is not drowned by the wave of the times, but remain purposeful towards the common goal.

The Church stands to gain from the general view on leadership, as we attempt to show what spiritual leadership should be like. In general, a good leader is supposed to have management skills. Today, we hear and read about the "transformational leadership model" (MacGregor Burns). It means, in summary, a combination of visionary thinking with change. This model suits Christian leadership a lot. A Christian spiritual leader is a transformational leader, creating an inspiring vision of heaven and seeing that his flock get there. Motivation and inspiration are important in his work of leading and directing, for an unmotivated Christian may not want to keep going.

As a visionary, the spiritual leader provides a strong and attractive depiction of the ultimate goal, providing direction, setting priorities, being proactive and involved, and not remaining satisfied at all with the way things are. This creates progress and dynamism. Once again, it is important that he or she makes the vision convincing and compelling. People not only need to have a feel of it, but also getting them to embrace it is very important. To achieve this, he or she provides a rich and interesting picture of the end in pursuit, how it will be when reached, and making its attainment a passion. He or she also makes it clear the attaining is a value shared by all, working up and inflaming all parties towards it. We motivate by making the shared vision worth attaining. One of the important questions would be: how can I inspire others to a realization of our common vision? Indeed, a true spiritual leader should be judged by his ability to inspire others to have passion for the common vision. Here, we are not limiting our discussion to priests alone. Often, it is what it takes a priest as a spiritual and pastoral leader that it takes any type of leadership in the Church to be successful.

For one to be a capable Christian leader, he or she should not allow the initial enthusiasm of the others to fade. Even in different circumstances the common vision should remain inspiring. Moreover, he or she should be able to connect the vision with the individual's needs, worries, and aspirations. In the Church, we can talk of sanctity vision and heavenly vision. Both are important for the Christian vision. We aspire to be holy, just as we aspire to go to heaven.

We hear of the expectancy theory. For instance, what is the need for constantly going to Church? Is it a need for Holy Communion? Is there an expectation of reward? What is the need to remain holy in all circumstances? All this will have to do with reward. Reward can be intrinsic and extrinsic. As one serves God, there is a feeling of good that goes with it. There is a natural joy in being a Christian. This can be regarded as intrinsic reward. There is also extrinsic reward. A good leader helps others to restate the vision on a daily basis and helps them to see it as more and more engaging through revisiting and restatement. Again, the good Christian leader has expert power, making him or her earn trust and credibility. He should be able to honestly and sincerely ask the people to listen to him and to follow him. This would then be followed by bonuses; that is encouragement. Encouragement can come through homilies and counselling. It can also come through assignment of tasks to members, as well as through recognition and gratitude. This is part of extrinsic reward. The ultimate extrinsic reward is heavenly bliss itself.

Management always plays a role in leadership and it is not different in spiritual leadership. We think of the leader as working for a group that has structures – we think of parish, diocese, the seminary, hospital, school, and so forth. We think of the Church as a whole. These are institutions within which Christians operate in, on a day-to-day basis. Each of these would have performance goals – performance goals of the parish, station, and so forth. Moreover, we all are supposed to have changed our lives and it matters how we manage it after the change. Here, the questions of coaching and training are of essence.

The competent spiritual and pastoral leader also sees that members have the necessary skills and abilities to play their part in evangelisation. Part of training is also giving and receiving feedback. In Christian training we have catechism and retreats (study and spiritual). Coaching also takes the form of homilies, personal consultation, and spiritual direction. What about the need for a team or teams that would help realise the goals, individuals' goals, and the common goal? Also to be looked for in the people are their vocation potentials, as well as the various gifts for serving God. Vocation to the priestly and religious lives can be looked out for. The spiritual leader as director sets the direction to be followed by "directee," although with due respect to the individual's freedom. He does the right thing even as he helps others to do the right thing, according to Eisenhower. To make progress towards the collectively held vision is essential. All this should be done both joyfully and excitingly.

4.1 Christ's Leadership Model

Above, we have just used normal leadership indices to look at pastoral and spiritual leadership. Who needs a model in leadership? "Every leader indeed," some would say. Christian leadership has a model and models. The greatest model in priestly and Christian leadership is Christ himself. We see this clearly in his teachings and in the way he leads. Christ's model of formation links leadership with the training of his successors, the apostles, who would carry on his work. Remarks here and there point to the fact that the first seminary was indeed Jesus' three-year encounter with his apostles. The confidence he had in sending them out to preach as he did confirms this. They had learnt through his words and examples. "He appointed twelve *to be with him*, and to be sent out to preach and have authority to cast out demon" (Mark 3:14–15). Our examination of Christ's leadership suffices for leadership in the Bible.

Christ's apostles needed to know his teachings through being with him. It takes the mind back to the old tradition of Elija and Elisha, with their band of apprentices (the school of prophets or sons of prophets). We also remember Moses and Joshua his assistant (Num. 27:18; Deut. 31). It is important to be with Jesus for one to be able to bear effective witness. "He who comes from heaven is above all... He bears witness to what he has seen and heard... For it is not by measure that he gives the Spirit" (John 3:31, 32, 34). Christ lived to bear witness to what he saw and heard and he would want his apostles to do the same.

Some of Christ's statements are directed towards his principles on leadership. Matt.20:25–26, "Jesus called them together and said, 'You know that the rulers of the Gentiles lord it over them, and their high officials exercise authority over them. Not so with you. Instead, whoever wants to become great among you must be your servant.'" A Christian leader has Jesus Christ's self-effacing character to imitate in Christian leadership. He or she should learn and understand what Christ meant when he said, "I am the Good Shepherd; the good shepherd lays down his life for his sheep" (John 14:6). Sacrifice is fundamental to Christ's model of leadership. This is unique in the sense that the life of the leader is involved. The seven "I am" of Jesus are known to do with life. Compared with the hired hand, the good shepherd is not there to put himself first, but the life of the sheep takes precedence. This says much about what a good priest's life should be – very antithetical to self-seeking.

The true shepherd leads the flock to the pasture. In the Christian sense, "pasture" is the "sheep food," as someone puts it, the Word of God. "Pasture" also means the Holy Eucharist, and all that would nourish especially the spiritual life. It is all about "raising." To better raise the sheep, one needs to learn about nutrition and nutrition techniques. One should learn about inadequate feed, diseases, and worms. Sheep food implies sheep health and welfare.

Christian leadership should be comforting to the sheep. The bible talks of "binding of wounds," which implies love, understanding, and compassion, Ps.147:3; Job 5:18. Some have referred to this as "applying the balm" or healing; the Christian leader soothes the wounds of those he or she serves. There are also the elements of correction and counselling as healing. These also amount to "strengthening the weak." Those who are confused and downcast and no longer see the goal as attainable are to be strengthened. Protection is another healing service rendered by the shepherd. There are likely to be predators out there, and the Christian leader is there to give security and allay fears. The shepherd knows the wolves, and what to do when they attack. Here, another very important quality of a Christian leader is humility – the humble shepherd. Maybe that was why in the Middle Ages, one of the conditions of admitting candidates to the seminary was that they should be of humble circumstances. This includes patience, and this is described as "washing of feet" (John 4:6). We sang in our primary school days: "He that is down needs fear no fall, He that is low no pride, He that is humble ever shall, Have God to be his guide" (John Bunyan).

Servant-hood is clear as a mark of Christ's leadership model. Beginning his public ministry, he condescended by allowing John the Baptist to baptise him, a teaching in submission and humility. Leadership is servant-hood. "Then Jesus came from Galilee to the Jordan to be baptized by John...." Matthew 3:13–15. David is identified as both shepherd and servant (Ezk. 34:23), shepherd after God's own heart (Jer. 3:15).

The spirit would then send Jesus out into the wilderness to be there forty days and nights. There, in the way he handles temptations, we have a lesson. The three forms of temptation he underwent seem to contain all possible temptations – to the flesh, materialism, and pride. This does not give room for excuses – "the devil tempted me." Jesus seems to be saying here that a true spiritual and pastoral leader should victor over temptations.

Everything about him is about preaching. He preached with power and preaching has to be clear and convincing, Mark 1:15. There is power in clarity and life-changing words and deeds. Why did he recruit simple people like fishermen, and people with understanding? He would want to begin with the fishermen and he brought a number of them for good working understanding, Matt.4. Look at the tax collectors, Matthew and Simon the zealot, also people of similar trade.

Another remarkable point is that Jesus was a person of authority and management, being in charge. He had control over evil spirits and gave them authority to leave those they held in bondage.

There are other forms of leadership in him – crisis manager, Mk. 1:30–31; man of prayer, Mk.1:35, Lk. 18:1. All this would be crowned by the fact that Jesus taught the importance of transfer of authority and empowerment, Mk. 1:40–45. His ministry was very much about that.

4.2 Leadership in the Fathers

In one of the early Fathers, St. Cyprian (c.200-c.258), we see an important reference to the Good Shepherd. In one of the letters he refers to Jesus' question to Simon Peter: "Do you love me? He replied: I do. He said to him: Feed my sheep." Cyprian notes the fact that Peter remained faithful to his words, "I do." According to him, "And we can see that these words were fulfilled by the very manner of his death, and the rest of the disciples acted likewise." St. Cyprian's words here remain relevant even in our day, and as long as ordination candidates go up the altar and pronounce "I do."

In one of his sermons, St. Gregory the Great (Pope; d.604) makes a depiction of pastoral leadership. "'Son of man, I have appointed you as watchman to the house of Israel.' Note that Ezekiel, whom the Lord sent to preach his word, is described as a watchman. Now a watchman always takes up his position on the heights so that he can see from a distance whatever approaches. Likewise, whoever is appointed watchman to a people should live a life on the heights so that he can help them by taking a wide survey" (Homily on Ezekiel, Lib.1,11, 406: CCL 142, 170–172).

St. Gregory reproaches himself that as a spiritual and pastoral leader he does not preach as he should, and that the life of a leader should follow adequately the principles that he preaches. If he fails, then it is "negligence." On the contrary, a spiritual and pastoral leader needs to be recollected. He talks of a particular responsibility of the leader – worry over the incursions of wolves who menace the flock entrusted to one's care. He himself sometimes meets with political authorities and helps to work for the preservation of rule of law. Is that not distracting? How does one combine the spiritual and pastoral with socio-political? He talks of doing justice to the sacred ministry of the word. What about the spiritually weak? He refers to the weaker sort of men who need to be attracted to the goal he desires for them. He talks of "lying back where I once was loath to stumble." He asks, "Who am I – what kind of watchman am I? I do not stand on the pinnacle of achievement, I languish rather in the depths of my weakness." "It is for love of him (redeemer of mankind) that I do not spare myself in preaching him," (*"pro cuius amore in eius eloquio nec mihi parco"*).

Another of the fathers, St. Bernard of Clairvaux (1090–1153), would comment on "How the Soul is Awakened and the Will Inspired to Seek God." What is necessary for a soul to aspire passionately to God is love, love that is the reason for searching. "For the love is the reason for the search, and the search is the fruit of love…." This surely would answer the question "how would the spiritual leader really succeed in taking someone to God?" He or she should help the person thirst for God (cf. Ps. 63; see also Song of Songs chp.3).

5. "The Spiritual Leadership of Archbishop Albert K. Obiefuna (A Tribute)"

Here, we are considering in a cursory fashion an African Christian who can be said to be a good model of spiritual and pastoral leadership. This tribute mirrors some spiritual leadership of a bishop whose life of witness really made a mark on his flock. He was a visionary and creative leader who promoted adoration of the Blessed Sacrament. So much that throughout the South-East of Nigeria and beyond, parishes have built Blessed Sacrament chapels separated from the parish Church.

Archbishop Albert K. Obiefuna was born in 1930 at Oraukwu, Anambra State, Nigeria. He had his primary school education in 1940–1947, andwent to All Hallows' (minor) Seminary, Onitsha, from 1951–57 and to Bigard Memorial Seminary in 1957–1959, and then to the Pontifical Urban University, Rome in 1959–1963. He was ordained as a priest in 1963. He studied further for his PhD in Theology and returned to Nigeria in 1967. He was the Parochial Vicar at the Holy Trinity Cathedral (now Basilica). At the end of the Nigerian civil war he taught at the Bigard Memorial Seminary Enugu, while running a parish at the same time. He became Rector of the seminary from 1976–1978 and was made bishop of Awka in 1978, Co-adjutor of Onitsha Archdiocese in 1994, and Archbishop of Onitsha on May 6, 1995. He died as Emeritus Archbishop of Onitsha in 2011.

The author of the tribute under review here saw him, worked with him, and was his priest and friend. Archbishop Obiefuna was this priest's bishop. "For me, in his meditations, the late Archbishop, emphasized among other things, five aspects of the purifying nature of suffering: endurance, hope, thankfulness, healing and forgiveness.... This is another spiritual leadership of Archbishop Obiefuna" (p. 10).

The tribute has the following chapters: 1. Profile of Archbishop Albert. K, Obiefuna 2. Why in America? (This tries to show why he died in the US where he went for treatment) 3. Spiritual Leadership of Archbishop Obiefuna 4. My encounter with the Archbishop 5. Bearing the Cross.

In page 11, we read, "The Archbishop left us a legacy of how to manage tensions in our lives by looking at the crucified Jesus Christ. The late Archbishop Obiefuna has left us with a legacy of life of prayer." In page 12, "... a praying Bishop, always on the kneeler before the Blessed Sacrament." "... a man of peace and reconciliation" In page 13. "... a man of truth with whom there is no falsehood". In page 19, "... I have a picture of him as a person that is very deep in reflection and thought." And in page 21,"He made God visible through his life... he invites each one of us to do the same".

The last statement says it all, "He made God visible through his life...." Spiritual leadership has it as one of its major burdens – making God visible, as the author puts it. People talk of making the invisible God visible. Christians know that that is what Christ is, the image of the invisible God (Col. I:15; see 1 Jn. 4:11–12).

6. Leadership in Seminary Courses

'The Priest, Pastor and Leader of the Parish Community' is the title of a Church document (2002) by the Congregation for the Clergy, and it looks like the title of a possible course in theology. Addressed to parish priests and collaborators involved in "cura animarum," it sounds very much like a course on the priest as leader, and I think that is what it really is. The document is clear that it is Christ's leadership that the priest as leader should

share in and imitate. In the summary of the document read at its presentation, (October 18, 2002) by Cardinal Dario Castrillon Hoyos, Prefect of
the Congregation, the document reads (in no.2): "What determines this
singular ecclesial centrality of the priest is the fundamental relation he has
with Christ, 'Head and Pastor, as his sacramental re-presentation.'"

Also, in *Pastores dabo vobis* (no.16) we read: "The priest's relation to
the Church is inscribed in the relation which the priest has to Christ, such
that the "sacramental representation" to Christ serves as the basis and
inspiration for the relation of the priest to the Church."

The priest has functions, "the liturgical proclamation of the Gospel and
the homily that follows it are both reserved to the priest" (no.4 *The Priest,
Pastor and Leader of the Parish Community: Introd.*). "Also the function
of guiding the community as shepherd, the proper function of the parish
priest, stems from his unique relation to Christ the Head and Shepherd"
(no.5 *The Priest, Pastor and Leader of the Parish Community: Introd.*). The
Church sees the priest the way Christ took his apostles, those who would
carry Christ's message to the ends of the world.

In the main body of the document, the following are listed as what the
priest, especially the parish priest, is there for – holiness, prayer, celebration of the Holy Eucharist, as well as for proclaiming the Word. Others
are: communion (*koinonia*), missionary commitment to evangelisation and
promotion of various forms of association. Such documents are inevitable
in priestly formation, knowing that they are aimed at addressing present
challenges.

7. Leadership in Formation

The formation in question is as outlined in *Pastores dabo vobis* – spiritual,
academic, human, and pastoral. We cannot forget preparation for celibate
lifestyle, which has been receiving particular attention by being singled out
and separated from the rest, although it is included in both spiritual and
human-social formation. However, it will not be enough if a priest is simply
a good celibate. He must add to it to other important priestly virtues. The
question; however, lends itself to serious attention: Does being simply a
good celibate make one a good priest? The question may arise from ongoing discussions about abuses in the priesthood.

A lot of documents are available: documents by the Church on priestly lifestyle. They are all based on the theological underpinnings of the teaching on priestly formation. There are also many available contemporary theories on leadership that are reflected in this write-up.

Concerning leadership and formation, priestly work has a lot to do with leadership. The leadership model of Jesus Christ will always take priority. Servant-leadership challenges formation of future priests in service. When we apply a transformational leadership model, seminarians should be formed to see the priesthood as a means of transforming lives. A spiritual leadership model enables seminarians to be taught to be spiritual leaders as Jesus; the spiritual leadership of Jesus Christ. How the seminary is run can also help to form the future priest in true leadership in the priesthood. Robert Donald Karpinski's, 'Leadership models for priestly formation in the Roman Catholic Church' (Jan. 1, 2001) is a research document on teaching of pastoral and spiritual leadership in the seminary. He proposes 1. the servant-leadership model, 2. a need to teach future priests to conquer self-interest and personal seeking, 3. discovering the person of Christ is proposed as a way to teach seminarians spiritual leadership, and 4. the work suggests the involvement of the lay people in formation. Such works would serve the purpose of available reading materials.

8. Some Suggestions

In spite of not being detailed enough, the following suggestions may still help in the discussion on raising the standard of formation.

1. It is important that students study the History of Seminary Formation. This may be lacking in some seminary formation curricula. Without doubting that it may be present in bits in various formation courses, it may still be necessary to make it an entirely independent course, because of its possible positive impact on future priests.

2. Why are people promoted to the priesthood? One of the reasons is that they have been judged knowledgeable and capable of the priestly lifestyle. Yet, there are many priests who seem to be ignorant of this. Some already ordained priests have claimed "the seminary offered little to prepare them for a life-time of celibate sexuality." As questionable as this allegation may be, priestly lifestyle should still find its way into

formation. Such a course or seminar should state details of what a priest's life should be, pointing out aids to correct living and factors that would militate against ideal priestly lifestyle.

3. One of the reasons candidates are promoted is that they are qualified for Church leadership. Church leadership seminars would need to be carried out during formation. While Pastoral Theology and Theology of Mission may have much leadership to offer the student, a separate and more practical seminar may be of inestimable help.

4. There may be need to take screening of seminarians more seriously. There are seminaries where there is too little contact with the rector. However high the population of seminarians, it is still necessary that the rector make time to discuss one on one with a candidate at least once a year. He would need to ask him about his family, his health, understanding of the priesthood, with its celibacy, poverty, and obedience. He would have to know if the candidate still has the right reason, intention, and personal consent for going into the priesthood.

5. After ordination, an annual mental check-up for priests may be necessary. This will surely help both body and soul. There has to be a way of helping every priest examine themselves mentally; to be followed up with some treatment where necessary.

6. It matters a lot how many seminarians are all together in a seminary. There should be a policy of control and putting a ceiling of between 250 and 300 seminarians per seminary. All this may be necessary considering the need for priests with the right conscience, not the emotionally ill-equipped, to serve in the priesthood.

7. In 1987, the Church in Nigeria issued *A Priest Forever*, a booklet of code of conduct for the Nigerian clergy. It serves as Vade Mecum and a reminder of the expectations the Church has of the priest in his daily life: "general guide-lines for the daily life and living patterns of the Nigerian priest." It has six major parts: a. Preamble, b. Christ the Priest, c. Christ the Prophet d., Christ the King e., Sanctions, and f. Conclusion. It treats the use of Church goods, avoidance of ostentation and wastage, further studies, celibacy, relationship with women, clerical dress, and so forth. Such documents that serve as a constant reminder are quite essential and very helpful. Since a high moral tone is in great demand in the work of

priests, no amount of reminders on this should be too much. This also calls for regular recollections and annual retreats.

9. Conclusion

One of the reasons strongly adduced as an explanation for priest abuse is cultural change. Since culture is said not to be static, it will also be necessary to study the times and the possible effect of such changes on priestly training. The Church needs to know when and how to adapt to the changing culture, as well as how to fortify formation against all threats.

Fitness of candidates matters a lot. If the wrong people are debarred from going in there, the priesthood will remain unsoiled. There is no doubt that the number of years in formation (6–9 years) is quite enough. Formators would need to devise means of really detecting the unsuitable candidates.

Often the issue in formation is not the lack of good principles or materials, but the lack of goodwill. The principal material of formation is the faith. The four arms of formation – spiritual, human, pastoral, intellectual – are all nothing if not imparted in the light of faith. For the laity as for the priest what is basic is faith in Christ. The various aspects of formation are only to help in living the faith in different circumstances of life.

However, it is possible to find many candidates who are involved in the "culture of dissent" (according to George Weigel). Such people are simply there, not wanting to imbibe formation, yet not wanting to leave. A bishop once said that the seminary should be made unbearable to such people, in such a way that on their own they would simply find their way out. This is challenging in the sense that one would not want to sacrifice the welfare of serious candidates in an effort to help unsuitable ones to leave. These problem candidates seem to be just waiting for ordination as the time to show their true colour. The other difficulty of it all is that they pretend to be serious with formation and are never found breaking any rule. Anybody in formation knows that that is one of the most difficult aspects of the work. In the end, no one should fail to realise the great importance of prayer both for formators and for "formandi."

Bibliography

Conrad W. Baars *The Role of the Church in the Causation, Treatment and Prevention of the Crisis in the priesthood*, 1971 (document).

Francis A. Oborji *The Spiritual Leadership of Archbishop Albert K. Obiefuna – A Tribute* (PDF document), 2011.

George Weigel *The Courage to be Catholic, Reform, and the Future of the Church* New York: Basic Books, 2002.

James Michael Lee & Louis J. Putz (eds) *Seminary Education in Time of Change* Notre Dame, 1965.

John Tracy Ellis *Essays in Seminary Education* Fides Publishers, 1967.

Philip Jenkins *The New Anti-Catholicism: The Last Acceptable Prejudice*, 2003.

Robert Donald Karpinski, *"Leadership models for priestly formation in the Roman Catholic Church"* Fordham University (Jan. 1, 2001).

Rose, Michael S. *Goodbye, Good men: How Liberals Brought Corruption into the Catholic Church Regnery* Publishing Inc., 2002.

Stafford Poole Seminary in Crisis New York, 1965.

Church Documents

Pope Benedict XIV *Sacramentum Poenitentiae*, 1741.

St. Pius X *Pascendi dominici gregis*, 1907.

Lumen gentium, 1964.

Presbyterorum ordinis, 1965.

Optatam totius, 1965.

Sacerdotalis caelibatus, 1967.

The Code of Canon Law, 1983.

Catechism of the Catholic Church, 1992.

Pastores dabo vobis, 1992.

Instruction Concerning the Criteria for the Discernment of Vocations with regard to Persons with Homosexual Tendencies in view of Admission to the Seminary and to Holy Orders , 2005.

John Chike Akunyili

Providing Enabling Environment for Lay Participation in Priestly Formation: A Personal Reflection

1. Introduction

A community is always blessed when they have a priest that is very compassionate and approachable. No more precious gift can be given to a community than a priest according to the heart of Christ. The Church's real evangelical battlefield is in the innermost minds of people, and their priests are invited to enter with tact and compunction, counting on the grace of God. The priests are those special people who will display the extraordinary ability to ignore some of the confusion, chaos, troubles and difficulties that surround them, and in obedience remain focused on whatever task that is at hand. A good priest shines a light that captures everyone within its boundaries.

To fully train a priest, we need to completely develop the four aspects of his life: physical, emotional, intellectual, and spiritual. The physical is nourished by good food and good medical care. The emotional is achieved mainly in the family and friends, while the institutions also handle the intellectual and spiritual components. This is the reason Jesus exclaimed: "I have come so that you will have life and have it abundantly" (Jn 10:10). This abundant life is holistic and not only spiritual. It includes also a state of physical and mental well-being. While the seminary as an institution provides the basic spiritual and intellectual contents of the seminary formation, these in themselves do not suffice for the holistic human person envisioned by Jesus. A person cannot be fully developed if he or she is only intellectually sound and spiritually deep. He or she has to be in addition, emotionally resilient, and physically sound as well. On these last two, the seminarian needs the support of the larger society, particularly the members of the Church.

2. Lay Participation in Priestly Formation

As lay Catholics, we have been called to manifest God's kingdom not only in the Church walls, but out in the world where we belong. Lay members of the Church, including lay professionals, tradesmen and women; doctors, nurses, engineers, layers, teachers, artisans, family members, friends, religious groups, etc. have a role to play in the formation of a priest. The priest's ministry is essentially with the people and for the people. It is clearly understood that not all to whom the priest is to minister are saints. Jesus was clear on this when he warned his disciples: "Behold I send you out as sheep among wolves...." (Matt 10:16). Sharing the experience of lay people in dealing with the wolves among themselves will make positive contributions to the formation of the would-be priest in his future dealing with the wolves even among the Christian laity. Therefore, without the input of lay people in the formation of the seminarian, it is conceivable that the priest might not be wholly formed to deal with issues that will arise in the course of his future ministry. This lay input does not necessarily have to come through formal lectures in classrooms but does not exclude it. Most of the influences could come from informal interactions and lay forums with seminarians in training.

Through baptism, we all – priests and lay people – have been sent to change the face of the world. God gave us weapons in form of talents and has called us to advance his kingdom wherever we find ourselves. God's spirit in us tells us to demonstrate God's love and one of the best ways to do that is to place our different talents at the disposal of these seminarians who gave up everything for the sake of Christ. Church's progress depends on the renewal of the priesthood. Laymen should then be professional missionaries and spread the light of hope via their talents, including their inputs in priestly formation of seminarians. It is, therefore, critical to provide the enabling environment for lay participation in the formation of would-be priests.

2.1 The Role of the Catholic Family

The family is the microcosm of the Church. In the family, God the father, the son and the Holy Ghost are represented by the father, the children and the mother in the family. The family is the cradle of vocation. Seminarians are the offspring of the laity and the family; supporting and nurturing vocation happens when parents teach their children Christian doctrines through words and actions. Families that pray together, practice love, humility, obedience, fear of God, etc., are more likely to produce a vocation. Families that initiate their children early in piety and devotion, in mass-serving, in loving and appreciating catholic life and action are likely to produce a seminarian.

Families should, therefore, expose their children early enough to the beauty of Church life, life of Christ, the beauty of the mass, the incense, the Church bells, catholic fellowship with their peers, and the joy of the priestly life. Families should show high respect to all those who have dedicated their lives to the service of the Church – teachers, catechists, nuns, priests, etc. Families should encourage their children once they feel the call, and not discourage them because they are their only son, daughter, etc. Once they enter the seminary, parents must be ready to sacrifice much, have patience, and endurance. Families will need to continue to pray fervently for the success of their child in the seminary. On the other hand, some parents want to have a family member become a priest at all costs. They pressure their child to enter the seminary, even when they know it is against his will. The vogue is to become *mama doctor, mama lawyer* or *mama father*. This should be discouraged as it could lead to frustrations on the part of the world-be priest. Families or even villages or Christian communities should desist from pressurising someone to enter the seminary or to continue his priestly formation by all means. This is because the priest ends up having a vocation of the mother, father, or even the community rather than his own call. This is the seed for future frustrations and lack of fulfilment of the priest, because the vocation was never his in the first place.

2.2 The Role of Parishioners

The community of worshippers has an important role in priestly formation. Hilary Clinton said once that it takes a village to raise a child, so too, it takes a village to nurture a seminarian (the priesthood). The community creates the environment for the seminarian's spiritual, emotional, and financial support. The community provides the prayerful environment for the spiritual growth of the seminarian as well as the moral environment for integral formation. Every lay member should know at least an individual seminarian and continue to pray for him until he is ordained. The leaders and members of different Church organisations must spread love, especially to our priests and seminarians. This Agape love binds us together, gives us meaning, validates our lives, and generates compassion.

Seminary training is tough. Seminarians are trained to love and to serve; to suppress and subdue their appetites, their pleasure, to mortify themselves; to be able to deal with the rich and the poor, the sick, and the depressed. They are trained to accept their likes and dislikes, to turn the other cheek, to witness to the truth, no matter how bitter. Seminarians can also often be enticed by the worldly values that constitute parameters of success in the secular world. They are also exposed to risks of relationship with the opposite sex and the rich and materialism. These constitute temptations that may come in very subtle ways. This is why the priest-to-be must have strong spiritual and moral formation. Without these, it is easy for the seminarian to forget the uniqueness of his call and become like the rest of men. Strong moral formation helps to establish the off-limits in his relationships with lay people of different categories.

I have alluded above on the importance of the financial contributions of the lay faithful to the formation of priests. Without the financial support of the laity, many of our priests today would not have made it to the priesthood. In the past, common people, market women, and teachers from poor countries in Europe sponsored seminarians in Africa. Even until now they have not stopped. Some of our people are learning to do the same. Religious societies in every parish – legion of Mary, sacred heart, knights of the Church, charismatic groups, youth organization, etc., – make their contributions to seminaries and postulants' houses for training of our future priests, sisters, and brothers. However, it is often the case that some are slow in contributing to the training of a seminarian because they fear he may not make it to the end. Fear of failure is out of place. Whether the candidate succeeds or fails does not matter, as you have made a worthy offering to God.

2.3 Lay Catholic Organizations

Catholic organizations like CMO, CWO, Catholic youths and knights can, as a group, adopt some seminarians. The reward defies words and is perhaps what Jesus had in mind when he said:

"He who receives a prophet in the name of a prophet shall receive a prophet's reward; and he who receives a righteous man in the name of a righteous man shall receive a righteous man's reward. "And whoever in the name of a disciple gives to one of these little ones even a cup of cold water to drink, truly I say to you, he shall not lose his reward" (Matt 10:41–42).

There is really a serious need for lay participation in priestly formation. A week in the seminary calendar could be devoted to interactions between aforementioned organisations and the seminarians. An Igbo proverb says: "*Onye bịara mmadụ nso, na-anụ isi eze ya.*" (It is only when you come near a person, that you can perceive his breath odour). When one comes closer to seminarians, he sees their needs. Engineers, for example, can initiate them into the rudiments of construction, as many of them will be faced with big construction projects in their parishes. I once visited Bishop Ekuwen at Uyo and met him in shorts, working with masons and iron benders. I was surprised to realise that he knows the ratio of sand, cement, and chippings that will produce the proper mixture for the decking and pillars of the building under construction.

Outstanding couples amongst the laity can talk to seminarians on the layman's perception of a priest or other relevant topics that will draw out the positive energy in the students. My wife of blessed memory and I tried this out with the Vincentian seminarians and the feedback was awesome. Even today, they clamour for such interaction.

3. The Example of Bigard Memorial Seminary, Enugu

When in 1978, Dr. Udora, Matron Udeze and I, among others, restarted the medical clinic at Bigard Memorial Seminary, at great cost to us, we had in mind this call to participate in the formation of priests. We wanted to put our professional skills to the service of the Church through the provision of healthcare services. We sought to make our modest contribution to the holistic formation of seminarians. Initially, this was difficult because many of the seminarians worried about many things. Worry, we know, is a darkroom in which negative things develop, and some students confided in us that the authorities would use their medical records to expel them from the seminary. To remedy this, we held a meeting with the formators and all agreed that the medical records of the seminarians, staff, and formators should be considered very confidential and off-limits. They could not be used to assess the fitness or otherwise of candidates for the priesthood. This was essential to building the confidence and trust of the seminarians on this voluntary medical team.

In response to our demand, the seminary authorities under the rectorship of PD Akpunonu welcomed the request and thus created an atmosphere of trust and confidence that facilitated our work. The rector loved the students, cared about their health concerns and loved what we were contributing to the seminary. He offered us a platform to talk to the students on important issues of health, and during our screening, we discovered some who had different types of ill health including Hepatitis B. We promptly got them immunised, thus making their life and priestly formation medically secure. As soon as this happened, there was an astronomical rise in the number of students visiting the clinics. The medical team now had to divide themselves into Monday, Wednesday, and Friday clinics to meet their medical demands.

The medical needs became so overwhelming that the visionary rector constructed a full-fledged hospital inside Bigard. Named St. Luke's Hospital, it had the full components of a theatre, out-patient clinics, admission wards, etc., and many students were surgically treated inside the seminary, thus saving time and resources. The facilities were so good that when Archbishop A.K. Obiefuna needed a minor surgery, he came and requested that I operate on him using the seminary theatre. Matron Udeze quickly got the theatre ready and we operated on him. The present rector, Fr. Theo Igwe, has upgraded the facility and it may in future serve as a referral centre for many other seminaries in the sub region.

This enabling environment was initiated by PD Akpunonu and was continued by his successors has saved a lot of money for the Church and has guaranteed good health for our teeming seminaries. This is one of the big benefits of living out "the priesthood of the laity." As of today, many doctors and nurses of different specialties work free of charge in many medical clinics in different seminaries. They also help guide the students emotionally. Emotions dull our senses and drown out ideas. Too often such students dwell on negatives and this weighs them down. When you properly handle their emotions, it helps them isolate the essential aims, and the inner untapped high-tensile strength in them is resurrected. They bubble with confidence and this properly sets them on their chosen course. Through our talents, we must radiate a genuine Catholic identity as we seek to heal, teach, serve, and lead as Jesus did. It is only through serving others that we can truly follow Jesus. Some seminarians may like to be doctors, lawyers, architects etc., but when they see those professionals take joy in serving them, it makes them understand their very unique position in the life of Christians and this energises them. It transforms their attitude and reignites their passion. As of today, the Bigard clinic can boast of the contributions of Dr. Anisiuba Emeka B, Prof. Meg Aghaji, Dr. Celestine Nweze, Prof. Ezeome Emma, nurses, physiotherapists, etc. We once more heartily thank the visionary rector – PD Akpunonu who created an enabling environment for this noble venture to succeed.

While the foregoing illustrates one formal way that lay people can participate in the formation of priests, there are also others who are engaged in providing one kind of service or the other. For example, cooks, drivers, gardeners, labourers and other domestic workers who dedicate their lives for small pay in the service of the Church, thereby making sure that the seminaries function without hitches. There are also lay people who are contributing financially in sponsoring seminarians. These are not only the rich and committed members of the Church but include also many poor members who throw in their widow's might, either as individuals or groups, to participate in material provisions for the seminarians. These contributions help to lift the financial burdens on the dioceses. In particular, it gives the contributors a sense of fulfilment that they are participating in the missionary work of the Church.

There are also others who are contributing in informal and less obvious ways in the training of the seminarians. Families host the seminarians during their long vacation apostolic work, which lasts for about six weeks or so. During this period, these families house and feed the seminarians or do so in conjunction with the parish zonal arrangement, whereby the members of the zones contribute to the feeding and other welfare needs of the seminarian posted to them. This is a great opportunity for the seminarian on formation to understand the people of God and work closely with them in spreading the Good News of Jesus Christ. It is always interesting when one sees a seminarian in cassock being led around the village by a catechist, members of the Legion of Mary, or Charismatic Renewal, in house-to-house visitation of Church members and even non-members to preach the word of

God to them. It affords the seminarian an opportunity to experience directly the difficulties of the people he will work with after his ordination, and to experience the material poverty of those who contribute to his up-keep. It is also a great opportunity for the community to make input into the training of the priest-to-be. The useful pieces of advice seminarians are offered during the period, the reports that are written about the seminarian on his performance during the period of apostolic work – all are crucial for the formation of the seminarian and important determinants of whether he is fit to continue or not.

It is usually the case that this report about the seminarian is written by the parish priest where the seminarian is posted for apostolic work. It would, however, be useful if lay members of the Church are allowed to express their views in a proper manner about the seminarian, his zeal and commitment to the ideals of the priesthood during the period of apostolic work. This is because the parish priest may be far away at the parish centre and may never be able to assess the seminarian properly due to lack of closeness and proper observation as much as the Church community itself does.

4. The Case of Dominic Cardinal Ekandem

Cardinal Ekandem's case clearly supports the need to have a fertile soil for the lay participation in seminary formation to thrive. He came from a rich family and the father was the chief of their place. Because he was to remain celibate, the father refused to have a hand in his training, believing that such would truncate the priestly ambition of this young and determined seminarian.

In 1942, he came together with Michael Eneja (later bishop of Enugu) and one Mr. Momoh (from Freetown) on apostolic work at coal camp Enugu. Julius Akunyili (my father) was the head of legion of Mary and it fell on him to find accommodation for the seminarians. He took them into his house at 13 Abagana Street and literally adopted them as his children. He saw to it that Ekandem finished his seminary training by providing all his financial needs. At this moment of writing, two seminarians still sojourn at that same room at coal camp, because my father reserved it just for seminarians. They are happy to be staying in a place that nurtured the likes of Cardinal Ekandem, Bishop Eneje, Msgr. Meze, etc.

Even today, the Akunyilis remain friendly with people, priests, and religious individuals from Ikot-Ekpene, because of all the lovely stories Cardinal Ekandem told them about Igbos and Akunyili family. In the book *"Cardinal Dominic Ekandem and the growth of the catholic Church in Nigeria"* the tributes paid to Akunyili family greatly enriched our souls. My father and the legion of Mary of 1942 fully understood the need to create a favourable environment for lay participation in priestly formation.

In page 136 of the book he states: "Although both bonds of marriage and religion fractured under the strain and stress of the war, Ekandem made conscious efforts to maintain the friendship he had formed with some Igbos. This was particularly true of his relationship with Akunyili family who had adopted Ekandem during his senior seminary years. Throughout the period of the war, Bishop Ekandem, who spoke Igbo with the proficiency of a native speaker, visited and supported them. The cardinal– then Bishop of Ikot-Ekpene, regularly crossed enemy boundaries to bring relief to us in our home town Agulu where we had taken refuge when Enugu fell. Through relief materials, etc. Bishop Ekandem ensured that his adopted family survived the civil war."

The above speaks for itself in terms of lay participation in priestly formation. If my father (the president of legion of Mary) had declined to Ekandem's school fees, his priestly ambition could have been aborted. This type of bond created in 1942 can still be replicated if lay faithful who can afford it adopt many needy seminarians as their sons. In my frequent visits to the seminary, I have come to realise that many cases similar to that of Cardinal Dominic Ekandem still exist.

5. Conclusion

In conclusion, I can state without equivocation that the laity has an enormous part to play in providing enabling environment for the formation of our priests. The greater the laity support, the richer the priestly harvest.

May the good Lord bless my parents who gave me such training that I regard anything Church as my comfort zone. We thank God for the life of PD Akpunonu who for 50 years has remained a great priest in the Lord's vineyard. May the good Lord continue to nourish him with the wisdom of Solomon and grant him more fruitful years in his journey of love and faith.

Luke Emehiele Ijezie

Strengthening the Faint-Hearted: The Prophetic Mission in Isaiah 40–55

1. Introduction

The search for a better life is a daily human quest. The biblical story is an account of God's constant efforts to better the lives of his people. The prophets, who were the special agents of the divine word, were called to participate in this mission. The prophetic mission of Deutero-Isaiah is presented as that of announcing divine comfort or consolation to God's people who found themselves in a life-threatening situation. God decides to bring them out of that situation and lead them as a shepherd to a place of greener pastures. This prophetic mission in this context involves the encouragement of the people to leave Babylon and return to Zion-Jerusalem to begin a better life in a divinely blessed environment. A very important aspect of this task is the liberation of the people from fear, which had crippled their resolve to receive the divine offer of freedom. The mission is better described as that of strengthening the faint-hearted and encouraging the weary of heart to embrace a better life of freedom and self-worth. This present essay focuses on how Deutero-Isaiah carries out the difficult task of strengthening the resolve of his frightened and frustrated people to accept the offer of divine love and salvation. This prophetic mission was not an easy one, and it is difficult to say to what extent he actually succeeded or failed in realising the goals of the mission. The prophet had to reckon with people who were victims of a paralysing fear that made them lose their courage just as they were victims of a type of cynicism that diminished their confidence in any emergent deliverer. This explains why the text of Isaiah 40–55 is filled with exhortations not to be afraid but to trust in the love and power of the deliverer, God. This essay is, however, not a detailed exegetical commentary on Deutero-Isaiah, which is hardly possible in a brief study of this nature.

The essay is in honour of the great biblical scholar, Professor Peter Damian Akpunonu, as he celebrates his golden jubilee as a Catholic priest. The choice of Deutero-Isaiah for this type of honour is guided by two considerations; first, Akpunonu has devoted much of his scholarly life to the study and teaching of the Bible, especially the works of Deutero-Isaiah. If the term biblical scholar has today almost become a household terminology in the Nigerian Church, this was not so before the 1970's. By the design of history and destiny, Akpunonu became one of the pioneers of serious biblical scholarship in Nigeria, as he finished his biblical studies in Rome in 1971, having passed through the Pontifical Biblical Institute (Biblicum) and the Pontifical Urban University (Urbaniana), all in Rome, with his doctoral research on the Prophet Isaiah, specifically on the theme of "Salvation in Deutero-Isaiah." His relatively recent book on the *Overture of the Book of Consolations [Isaiah 40:1–11]*[1] speaks volumes of the depth of research he has devoted to Deutero-Isaiah. Secondly, the mission of Deutero-Isaiah sums up the apostolate of P.D. Akpunonu as a priest, scholar and prophetic leader at various levels. Paradoxically, his apostolate has always been that of salvaging situations and people through an extraordinary gift of transformational leadership. Just like his anonymous mentor, Deutero-Isaiah, Akpunonu has been exceptional in his commitment to the work of consoling and strengthening people and the mission of uplifting the weary and faint-hearted. His has been 50 eventful years of priestly apostolate that has left significant footprints on the sands of the local and universal Church. It is, therefore, most appropriate that an essay on Deutero-Isaiah, one of the finest works of the biblical text, should be devoted to this our great formator and mentor.

2. Profile of Isaiah 40–55: Unity and Setting

The book of Isaiah, since the study of B. Duhm in 1892,[2] has been recognised to consist of three major parts: 1–39 (First Isaiah, attributed to Isaiah of Jerusalem), 40–55 (Deutero-Isaiah, attributed to a prophet of the late exilic period), and 56–66 (Trito-Isaiah, considered a prophetic work of the post-exilic period). There is, however, much debate regarding this division as many elements overlap in the three parts. One finds, in the current

---

1 P. D. Akpunonu, *The Overture of the Book of Consolations [Isaiah 40:1–11]* (New York: Peter Lang, 2004).
2 B. Duhm, *Das Buch Jesaja übersetzt und erklärt* (Gottingen [4]1922).

research in Isaiah, a greater tendency to argue for the unity of the whole book, at least at the redaction level, as the entire corpus is seen as a product of a progressive and complex literary development.[3]

The author of the section 40–55 remains anonymous, but scholars commonly refer to both this author and the work as Deutero-Isaiah (=Second Isaiah). The same approach is adopted in this essay even though it is most likely that the work is a product of a group of authors.[4] This is shown by some divergences of thought and style within the section. There is also the corpus of texts in 40–55 traditionally regarded as the four Servant Songs. These Songs are found in 42:1–4; 49:1–6; 50:4–9 and 52:13–53:12. While some scholars consider the Songs as originally independent units before their insertion into the text of Deutero-Isaiah,[5] many others dispute their independent existence, seeing them as being composed by the same author/authors of Deutero-Isaiah.[6] Most modern scholars adopt the second position as they consider the Songs integral to the ideas of Deutero-Isaiah.

---

3 See R. E. Clements, "A Light to the Nations: A Central Theme of the Book of Isaiah," in *Forming Prophetic Literature. Essays on Isaiah and the Twelve in Honor of John D. W. Watts* (eds. J. W. Watts and P. R. House; JSOTS 235; Sheffield 1996) 57–69; J. Blenkinsopp, *A History of Prophecy in Israel* (Revised and Enlarged Edition; Louisville 1996) 182–185; ID, *Isaiah 1–39. A New Translation with Introduction and Commentary* (AB 19; New York: 2000) 83–92.

4 According to Rainer Albertz (*A History of Israelite Religion in the Old Testament Period, Volume 2: from the Exile to the Maccabees* [Original in German, Göttingen 1992; London: SCM Press Ltd., 1994] 415), "by Deutero-Isaiah we can understand a group of theologians gathered round a master which came from circles of descendants of the temple singers and cult prophets of the Jerusalem temple with their nationalistic attitude, and was intensively concerned with the prophecy of Isaiah."

5 This first position was first advocated by B. Duhm in his study, *Das Buch Jesaja*, published in 1892, and was later adopted by a number of scholars. For the discussion, see C. R. North, *The Suffering Servant in Deutero-Isaiah. An Historical and Exegetical Study* (Oxford 1948); C. Stuhlmuehler, "Deutero-Isaiah: Major Transitions in the Prophet's Theology and in Contemporary Scholarship," *CBQ* 42 (1980) 1–29.

6 For this second position, which sees the Songs as integral to the book, see T. D. N. Mettinger, *A Farewell to the Servant Songs. A Critical Examination of an Exegetical Axiom* (Regiae Societatis Humaniorum Litterarum Ludensis Scripta Minora; Lund, 1983); A. Wilson, *The Nations in Deutero-Isaiah. A Study on Composition and Structure* (Ancient Near Eastern Texts and Studies

The closer one reads the Songs, the clearer one discovers their literary affin-
ity with the rest of the corpus of Isaiah 40–55. However, the text (40–55)
has a very complex structure and that explains why most interpreters differ
in their views regarding its unity.

The text of Isaiah 40–55 is set within the context of the events of the
final days or years of the Babylonian empire. The then ruling emperor in
Babylon was Nabonidus who had grown weak and very unpopular. At the
same time Cyrus, the Persian King, was conquering all the territories and
kingdoms around. He marched on Babylon in 539 B.C. and captured it
without much battle. This marked the end of the neo-Babylonian empire
and the beginning of the Persian empire. In 538, Cyrus is reported to have
issued an edict allowing the Jewish exiles to return to their native land,
and more significantly to rebuild the temple of YHWH (Yahweh) in Jerusalem. This is reported in 2 Chron 36:23; Ezra 1:1–1; 6:3–5. It is not clear
whether the text of Deutero-Isaiah was written before or after the events of
the final conquest of 539 B.C. and edict of 538. Although the text does not
specifically mention any of them, the tone of the author in some sections is
that of one already certain of the fall of Babylon and the magnanimity of
Cyrus to let the exiles return to Zion-Jerusalem. It is, therefore, difficult to
be certain about the precise date of composition. What is clear is that the
text is set within these historical circumstances. Again, there is a marked
difference between the tone of chapters 40–48 and 49–55, seemingly pointing to diverse dates of composition. While the thought world of 40–48
reflects the tone of expectation of freedom for the Babylonian exiles, the
contents of 49–55 reflect the mood of rebuilding Zion-Jerusalem, the holy
city. However, the text was written with the aim of instigating the desire
for freedom in the Israelite exiles in the Babylonian empire and also of
convincing those still in doubt that the new era has better promises than
the status quo in Babylon. It is the opinion of most scholars that the exiles
in Babylon were economically comfortable, having acquired much wealth
in the foreign land. This made it difficult to convince them to return to the
poverty-stricken land of Judah, where they were not even sure of a warm
welcome. For them, returning to Judah meant returning to the past with

1; New York 1986) 250–317; Blenkinsopp, *A History of Prophecy in Israel*,
182–193.

all its dangers. The author devotes a lot of words praising Cyrus, the new Persian king, and also trying to convince his reluctant audience that the King means well and that he is actually the agent of Israel's God, YHWH.

In terms of form, the text of Isaiah 40–55 is presented as a salvation oracle that is clearly stated in every part of the text. Claus Westermann identifies the whole of 40–55 as a proclamation of salvation, all concentrated on Israel's liberation from Babylonian captivity.[7] In this, he considers the text as the only complex of oracles of salvation in the Old Testament, whose historical context can be dated with some certainty.[8] Akpunonu makes an elaborate analysis of the genre of Salvation Oracle together with that of Announcement of Salvation, both of which he identifies in Isaiah 40–55.[9] While Salvation Oracle refers to a direct saving response to a distress call, the Announcement of Salvation is a message given to a group regarding a salvation that will come in the future.[10]

3. Mission of Liberation from Fear

Deutero-Isaiah was sent to encourage a faint-hearted people who were crippled by the fear of superior and uncanny forces around them. This fear gnawing at the very core of the people's being is intensified by their conviction that YHWH had withdrawn from them. The consequence was the fear of human powers and diverse forms of oppressive forces. This is clearly expressed in Isa 51:12–13:

> "I, it is I who comfort you. Can you then fear (*yr'*) mortal man, who is human only, to be looked upon as grass, and forget YHWH, your maker, who stretched out the heavens and laid the foundations of the earth? You fear (*phd*) continually all day long because of the fury of the oppressor, as he makes ready to destroy. But where is the fury of the oppressor?"

The two Hebrew verbs rendered here as "fear" are *yārē'* and *pahad*, both of which occur frequently in Deutero-Isaiah. The verb *yārē'* occurs 333 times in the Old Testament with such senses as "to fear, honour, respect,

---

7   C. Westermann, *Prophetic Oracles of Salvation in the Old Testament* (Original in German 1987; ET: Edingurgh: T & T Clark, 1991) 39.

8   Westermann, *Prophetic Oracles of Salvation*, 39.

9   Akpunonu, *The Overture*, 40–44.

10 Akpunonu, *The Overture*, 41–43.

worship,"[11] all depending on the context. It can express the positive sense of fear as in reverence of God or the negative sense of dread of terrifying things. It is used in this negative sense in Isa 51:12 and many other places in 40–55, where it is used synonymously with *phd*. This verbal root *phd* occurs 25 times in the Old Testament, expressing "the shaking that can result from either extreme terror or joy."[12] In the present case of 51:13, the Prophet uses it to express the trembling or dread that comes as a result of a terrible oppression.[13] The fear of oppressive forces is mostly a consequence of insufficient faith in the protective power of YHWH.

Deutero-Isaiah takes up the mission to elaborate on YHWH's special benevolence towards his people and why the people should abolish every form of fear and embrace the new life of freedom in YHWH's presence. In this state of affairs, the main mission of the Prophet is expressed in Isa 40:1 in the words: "Comfort, O comfort My people!" The main terminology here is the Hebrew verb *niham*, repeated two times in the Piel imperative plural form (*nahamu*), with the sense of comforting, consoling, encouraging or strengthening. In this context, it has the sense of strengthening or comforting a people whose greatest ailment is fear. It also involves relief from distress, invigoration, and restoration.[14] But who is to give this kind of comfort? Is the prophet really the one commanded to give the comfort? Since the command to comfort the people is in the plural, there is the question whether the agents of the comforting are many. Who are these addressees commanded to comfort the people? There is much discussion of this crux among scholars.[15] Following the context and ancient belief of the people of the time, it is most probable that God is addressing the divine assembly. The prophet is the one who announces the proceedings of the assembly. In other words, Deutero-Isaiah is the announcer or herald of the comfort which God himself is bringing to his people. Deutero-Isaiah recognises that fear is the great obstacle militating against the divine plan of freedom for the people. This fear is so overwhelming that it has caused the people to

---

11 M. V. Van Pelt and W. C. Kaiser, Jr., "*yr,*'" *NIDOTTE* 2, 527.
12 M. V. Van Pelt and W. C. Kaiser, Jr., "*phd,*" *NIDOTTE* 3, 597.
13 Van Pelt and W. C. Kaiser, *NIDOTTE* 3, 597.
14 Akpunonu, *The Overture*, 83.
15 See the detailed discussion in Akpunonu, *The Overture*, 80–84.

lose confidence both in God and in themselves. The liberation from fear becomes a mission. Bruna Costacurta explains that the overcoming of fear in the biblical presentation usually comes, first, through the intervention of an external force presented as capable of bringing about the rescue, and secondly, through a new presentation of the reality causing the fear.[16] Deutero-Isaiah helps the people to overcome their fear by exposing the causes of the fear, demystifying them and pronouncing reassuring words of salvation from YHWH. The text is thus filled with the exhortation not to fear, and this is repeated many times and developed on diverse levels. These levels need further elaboration.

3.1 Liberation from Fear Caused by Guilt-Complex

The first aspect of the people's fear that the text addresses is their distress caused by guilt complex. The exile carried with it a great sense of guilt as the people were convinced that if YHWH could allow them and their fathers to suffer such shame, his grievances and anger against them must have been very serious. Many of the interpretations of the exile attribute it to sin. Some other interpretations wonder how the divine justice could be so ruthless. If the people are bogged down by a guilt complex, YHWH opens a new chapter of total reconciliation. In fact the Prophet is commissioned to announce it: "Speak tenderly to Jerusalem and proclaim to her that her service is at an end, her guilt is expiated; indeed she has received from the hand of YHWH double for all her sins" (40:2). The prophet is mandated to "speak to the heart of Jerusalem," which means that the whole proclamation is not one of condemnation but soothing words that uplift the heart. YHWH recognises the psychological state of his distraught people and announces healing through reconciliation. The prophet himself initially appears reluctant to make the announcement, but he is encouraged not to

---

16 B. Costacurta, *La vita minacciata. Il tema della paura nella Bibbia Ebraica* (Analecta Biblica 119; Rome: Editrice Pontificio Biblico, 1988) 257–267. As Costacurta (257) puts it, "Quando l'uomo é sotto la minaccia, la sua paura puó essere vinta dall'intervento di un altro che si presenti come capace di soccorrere e salvare. Con l'invito a non temere, o con un segno destinato a fondare la fiducia, l'uomo impaurito viene cosí aiutato a guardare con occhi diversi il pericolo e a ritrovare la capacitá di affrontare il proprio timore e di suprarlo."

fear to cry out this message (40:9) as YHWH is now out to gather together his scattered people as a shepherd gathers his flock (40:10–11).

One learns from Ezekiel 37 that the exiles in Babylon were dry bones that regained vitality through the prophetic word. Here, Ezekiel dramatises the passage of the Jewish nation from death to life. As André LaCocque puts it: "The death of the nation in Babylon is no mere chastisement; the exile is no sleep, no parenthetical time, no transient night before morning comes, and still less the feigned decease of an initiate. The exile is no sleep; it is death, death without morrow."[17] In this real death situation, Deutero-Isaiah, just like Ezekiel, also employs the word of God to revitalise his moribund people. He announces the inauguration of a new era which sounds like a new creation. The people are asked to embrace the new era that YHWH is now opening up for them. "Remember not the events of the past, the things of long ago consider not. See, I am doing something new!" (43:18–19). This new thing is frequently repeated in the text. Deutero-Isaiah's mission can be likened to the mission of Moses in Egypt, when he was commissioned to tell Pharaoh: "Let my people go!" In Deutero-Isaiah, Israel is called back to the beginning to begin a new history. This is the new thing that YHWH is doing. The people should return to Jerusalem and begin a new and glorious life as free people in YHWH's presence. It is regarded as a Second Exodus and the pathways are likened to the desert of the exodus wanderings. "In the desert I make a way, in the wasteland, rivers" (43:19). There is a glorious imagery drawn in 55:12–13:

> "For you will go out with joy and be led forth with peace. The mountains and the hills will break forth into shouts of joy before you, and all the trees of the field will clap their hands. In place of the thorn-bush, the cypress shall grow, instead of nettles, the myrtle. This shall be to YHWH's renown, an everlasting imperishable sign."

The people have to experience the desert in a new way (see also 40:3–5; 43:19–20) and re-enter into a new land of more lasting freedom and peace (51:3). In view of this new thing, the people are encouraged not to fear: "Fear not for I have redeemed you" (43:1).

---

17 A. LaCocque, "Ezekiel 37:1–14: From Death to Life," in *Thinking Biblically. Exegetical and Hermeneutical Studies* (A. LaCocque and P. Ricoeur; Chicago and London: University of Chicago Press, 1998) 146.

3.2 Liberation from Fear Caused by Sense of Divine Abandonment

Deutero-Isaiah addresses the situation of people in a deep crisis of faith, people who have gone through horrible experiences in life and are being tortured by a collective sense of divine abandonment. This collective sense of divine abandonment is alluded to in many places, one of which is in 49:14–15: "But Zion said, 'YHWH has forsaken me, my Lord has forgotten me.' Can a woman forget her nursing child and have no compassion on the son of her womb? Even these may forget, but I will not forget you." Here, the author draws analogy with the mystical union between a mother and her child in the womb, meaning that YHWH is so intrinsically linked to his people that he can never abandon them.

The sense of being abandoned and not being loved anymore is a terrible sensation. When religious people find themselves in this existential crisis, they usually run to God for succour and accompaniment. It becomes a disastrous experience, when this divine accompaniment is no longer forthcoming or no longer felt. The sense of divine abandonment is a near death experience. The expression "abandoned by God," according to Paul Ricoeur, "imposes a theological stamp on all suffering. All suffering is in this way designated, not just as suffering before God, but, in truth, owing to God."[18] The exilic experience had shattered Israel's sense of security and hope of greatness in YHWH's presence. Most of the people had lost confidence in YHWH's power to deliver for his people, as they felt they had languished for years in exile without any divine succour. Akpunonu expresses it succinctly:

> "The exile raised a volley of questions: Why did Yahweh abandon and sell his people for nothing [Isa 50:1; 52:3]? Why did he commit his temple to flames? Was Yahweh unwilling or unable to defend it? If unwilling, what became of his unconditional love, of his solemn promises, oaths which he swore by his very self [Gen 22:16–18]? Could Yahweh then perjure himself? If unable, then Marduk, not Yahweh was God."[19]

Faced with perplexities, such as these, the people were now in doubt of YHWH's credibility, and many resorted to idolatry. The popular belief was

---

18 Paul Ricoeur, "Lamentation as Prayer," in *Thinking Biblically*, 221–222.
19 Akpunonu, *The Overture*, 21.

that either YHWH had abandoned his people or that he was incapable of rescuing them. Thomas L. Laclerc qualifies it as a theological crisis, which can be expressed as: "Can God's word be trusted?"[20] One of the main thrusts of the text of Deutero-Isaiah is the affirmation that YHWH's powerful presence is everywhere, no matter the condition. There is nothing as reassuring as the words: "Fear not for I am with you" (43:5). As long as YHWH's presence remains with her, Israel has no need to fear:

> "But now, thus says YHWH, who created you, O Jacob, and who formed you, O Israel: Fear not for I have redeemed you. I have called you by name: you are mine. When you pass through the water, I will be with you; in the rivers you shall not drown. When you walk through fire, you shall not be burned; the flames shall not consume you" (43:1–2).

The Prophet goes on to reassure his people of the solidity of YHWH's love for them. Here, he presents a very touching and emotional proclamation of divine love: "Because you are precious in my eyes you have been honoured, and I love you and I shall set mankind (*adam*) in exchange for you and nations for your life" (43:4). The text aims to restore the people's confidence in YHWH's immense love for them and their great worth in his eyes, despite the disgrace of the exile. The catastrophe of the exile had radically battered the people's faith both in the present and in the future, just as it had brought their self-esteem to its lowest ebb. Despite Israel's low self-esteem, YHWH calls her his servant and his darling: "Fear not, O Jacob, my servant, the darling whom I have chosen" (44:2). The whole text of Deutero-Isaiah is, in fact, a love message from YHWH to Israel. It contains many wonderful words that have become the favourite of lovers all over the world. Typical are these reinvigorating divine words to Israel in 54:10: "Though the mountains leave their place and the hills be shaken, my love shall never leave you nor my covenant of peace be shaken, says YHWH, who has compassion on you."

---

20 T. L. Laclerc, *Introduction to the Prophets. Their Stories, Sayings, and Scrolls* (New York: Paulist Press, 2007) 308.

3.3 Liberation from Fear Caused by Crisis of Faith in YHWH's Power to Save

If the question of YHWH abandoning his people can be contradicted, there is the other question of YHWH's very power to save. Has YHWH the power to save his people? The people had grown used to the notion that the Israelite national deity was impotent, having presumably proved himself incapable before the Babylonian rulers and Babylonian gods. The author of Isaiah 40–55 takes it as a duty to respond to these allegations and doubts. It is from this point of view that one can see the coherence of the text's complex elaborations of YHWH's power and the powerlessness of idols and foreign gods. There is this challenging poser in 44:7: "Who is like me? Let him stand up and speak, make it evident, and confront me with it." YHWH is presented as the supreme Lord of creation and universal ruler. As long as Israel holds fast to YHWH, no principality or power can suppress her. "Yes, from eternity I am He. There is none who can deliver from my hand. I work, and who can reverse it?" (43:13). This statement ("There is no one who can deliver from my hand" – 'ēn mîyyadî maṣṣîl) has been interpreted by Aaron Chalmers as a set formula which, when found with the deity, expresses God's power and incomparability.[21] "Yahweh's might is such that no one is able to escape from the deity's grasp once captured, in other words, no one is the deity's equal."[22]

The argument of YHWH's power and incomparability is presented in various forms in the text, but Rainer Albertz sums it up in three points: "it was not the world powers but Yahweh who ruled world history in a sovereign way [Isa.40.12–17]; it was not strange gods but Yahweh who sat in government [vv.18–24]; it was not the Babylonian star gods but Yahweh who determined fate [vv.25–26]."[23] Albertz picks up the three points from Isaiah 40, which is the opening chapter of Deutero-Isaiah, and encapsulates the main arguments of the corpus.

The power of YHWH is presented in a way to convince the reluctant exiles that the divine accompaniment will lead them securely home to their

---

21 A. Chalmers, "'There is No Deliverer [from My Hand]'– A Formula Analysis," *VT* 55 (3, 2005) 287–292.
22 Chalmers, "There is No Deliverer," 292.
23 Albertz, *A History of Israelite Religion*, 416.

own land. For those who are in doubt and prefer to stay in Babylon for fear of not having enough strength to leave, the prophet highlights the power of YHWH in contrast to the pagan gods:

> "Do you not know or have you not heard? YHWH is the eternal God, creator of the ends of the earth. He does not faint nor grow weary, and his knowledge is beyond scrutiny. He gives strength to the fainting; for the weak he makes vigour abound. Though young men faint and grow weary, and youths stagger and fall, they that hope in YHWH will renew their strength, they will soar as with eagles' wings. They will run and not grow weary, walk and not grow faint" (40:28–31).

Deutero-Isaiah makes these elaborate arguments on the power of YHWH, in order to convince his audience to accept the divine proposal of restoration and new life.

3.4 Liberation from Fear of Enemies and Oppressors

There was the fear among the people that any manifest desire on their part to seek for freedom would be disastrously crushed by the ruling powers, and there was no other human or divine force to rescue them from such fury. It was people tremendously demoralised and resigned to fate. Deutero-Isaiah addresses this fear as he allows the people to understand the superior power of YHWH over human powers. The fear of oppressive forces is mostly a consequence of insufficient faith in the protective power of YHWH. As the text of 51:13 says, the people were in constant dread of the fury of the oppressor. This made it difficult to convince them that freedom was a better option. They needed to be convinced that YHWH was willing to protect them, and this is what Deutero-Isaiah labours to achieve, as in these words:

> "Thus says YHWH: Can booty be taken from a warrior? Or captives be rescued from a tyrant? Yes, captives can be taken from a warrior, and booty be rescued from a tyrant. Those who oppose you I will oppose, and your sons I will save. I will make your oppressors eat their own flesh, and they shall be drunk with their own blood as with the juice of the grape. All mankind shall know that I, YHWH, am your saviour, your redeemer, the Mighty One of Jacob" (49:24–26).

The prophet encourages them not to fear the reproaches of human beings and their reviling, as YHWH's saving justice would soon prevail (51:7). This saving justice will establish them on a pedestal, where the oppressor cannot reach, and that will bring about the end of the fear of oppression (54:14). The prophet sums it up by saying that the destroyer has no real power over

YHWH's people, since both the destroyer and his weapons are all under YHWH's power and control (54:16). Given this scenario, Deutero-Isaiah reassures the people with these often quoted words: "No weapon fashioned against you shall prevail; every tongue you shall prove false that launches an accusation against you. This is the lot of the servants of YHWH, their vindication from me, says YHWH" (54:17).

4. Some Lessons for the Contemporary Audience

The text of Isaiah 40–55 presents many interesting lessons for the modern reader. Two of such lessons relate to the theme of fear and the role of the prophetic word. In both, Deutero-Isaiah shows the way in his mission of strengthening the faint-hearted through the agency of the divine word.

Fear is usually a constraining factor in the daily quest for a better life, and sometimes it is so overwhelming that the desire to strive is quenched. In the case of Israel, the long exilic experience had created a fearful mind-set that was difficult to eradicate. The people were in constant dread of oppressors, and this also influenced their religious fidelity. The contemporary religious life is menaced by the fear provoked by a myriad of forces, such as hostile supernatural forces, human terror and other ideological factors. These factors have diverse influences on religion, depending on the perception of the particular culture or society. In most African contexts, the fear of supernatural forces and human oppressors has created a myriad of religious sects and religious modes of acquiring power. This has brought about much fetishism and syncretism in the practice of the Christian faith. Pastors of soul are often at a loss how to help their harassed and timid flock.

Deutero-Isaiah presents the word of God as a powerful force for the liberation of people from fear. The word exposes the greater power of God in the face of the dreadful things that provoke fear in people. The word functions by demystifying the powers attributed to these fear-provoking phenomena. In the African context, there is an increasing rediscovery of the power of the word, but the challenge is to devise better ways of exposing and interpreting this word, so that it actually succeeds in addressing the religious and existential fears of the harassed masses. From this point of view, one cannot but remain grateful to scholars like P. D. Akpunonu, who have spent their lives and resources to the study and exposition of the word of God. "They will see the glory of YHWH, the spendour of our God. Strengthen the hands that are feeble, make firm the knees that are weak, say to those whose hearts are frightened: Be strong, fear not! Here is your God, he comes with vindication, with divine recompense he comes to save you" (Isa 35:2–4).

5. Conclusion

This essay has addressed the theme of fear, which is intrinsic to the mission of Deutero-Isaiah. This mission is aptly captured in the topic of this essay as that of strengthening the faint-hearted. It is a mission to encourage the Israelite exiles in Babylon to return home. The people were not very eager to leave, as they were afraid of both the known and unknown forces that could make their situation worse. The prophet devotes a lot of argument to this collective fear, making clear the point that the power and love of YHWH will always accompany them. The prophet demonstrates the power of the word of God in effecting the liberation from fear.

Emmanuel U. Dim

Preaching the Gospel Without Ceasing: Jesus' Enduring Commission to His Disciples (Matt 28,16–20)

(An Exegetical Reflection for the Priestly Golden Jubilee of Rev. Fr. Prof. P.D. Akpunonu)

1. Introduction

Jesus came into the world to save the world. He brought to mankind the good news of salvation. Through Jesus we have come to know God, for he is the Son of God. He was "in the beginning" with God and through him all things were made (John 1, 1–3).[1] Jesus preached the gospel throughout his ministry on earth. After his resurrection and before his ascension, he commissioned his disciples to continue this preaching to all nations (Matt 28, 16–20).

The Church, right from its very beginning, has remained faithful to this commission. The Acts of the Apostles, all the letters of St. Paul and, in fact, the entire NT bears testimony to this fact. Paul's missionary journeys, during which he passed through uncountable difficulties and challenges, were undertaken for this purpose. Hence he himself emphasises: "Woe to me if I do not proclaim the gospel" (1 Cor 9, 16). He also strongly urges Timothy to always preach the Gospel, insisting on it in season and out of season, so as to patiently convince, reproach and encourage the People of God (2 Tim 4,1–2).

2. The Commissioning of the Disciples by Jesus

That Jesus commissioned his disciples to preach the gospel to all nations is amply documented in the gospel accounts and in the entire NT (cf. Mark 16,14–18; Luke 24,36–49; John 20,19–23 and Acts 1,6–8). For conciseness,

---

1   All biblical citations in this write up will be taken from the New Revised standard version.

we shall dwell mainly on the account of Matthew, as already signalled by the title of this article. From here, we shall make allusion, if necessary, to the other accounts.

This "commissioning" is recorded by Matthew in 28, 16–20, as already indicated. This text could be divided into two major parts: a) the appearance of the risen Jesus to his disciples and the assertion of his authority (Matt 28, 16–18), and b) the commission of Jesus to his disciples and the promise of his abiding presence (Matt 28, 19–20.[2]

Thus, this commissioning by Jesus took place after his resurrection from the dead (Matt 28, 1–20). After Jesus' death and burial on Good Friday, the Sabbath day (the day of rest for the Jews) also came and passed. Then on the first day of the week, the Sunday, Mary Magdalene and "the other Mary" – the two Marys who had witnessed his burial (Matt 27, 61) – went "to see the tomb" (Matt 28, 1) where Jesus was buried, as part of the homage which they were paying to him.[3] A sudden earthquake and the surprising appearance of an angel were their stunning experience. After calming them down and assuring them that Jesus had risen from the dead (Matt 28,1–6), the angel then said to them: "Then go quickly and tell his disciples 'he has been raised from the dead, and indeed he is going ahead of you to Galilee; there you will see him.' This is my message for you" (Matt 28,7).

As the manifestly frightened women ran with great joy to deliver this message of the angel to the disciples, Jesus suddenly met them. In their fright but great joy, they came to him, took hold of him and worshipped him (Matt 28, 9). Jesus calmed them down and gave them the same message that the angel had earlier given to them, saying: "do not be afraid; go and tell my brothers to go to Galilee; there they will see me" (Matt 28, 10).

It is clear that the women acted according to the instructions of both the angel and the risen Jesus. Hence, Matt 28, 16–20 records what actually transpired when the eleven disciples finally gathered in Galilee, on the mountain to which Jesus had directed them. In fact, this their final meeting with Jesus on this mountain has fulfilled Jesus' promise at the Last Supper to "go ahead" of the disciples "to Galilee" (Matt 26, 32), the message of

---

2   D. SENIOR, *Matthew* (Abingdon New Testament Commentaries; Nashville: Abingdon Press, 1998) 345.
3   SENIOR, *Matthew*, 340.

the angel to the women at the empty tomb (Matt 28,7), and the risen Jesus' own instructions to the women (Matt 28,10).[4] When they saw Jesus, they worshipped him, even though some doubted. It was then that Jesus came to them and officially commissioned them saying: "All authority in heaven and on earth has been given to me. Go therefore and make disciples of all nations, baptising them in the name of the Father and of the Son and of the Holy Spirit, and teaching them to obey everything that I have commanded you. And remember, I am with you always, to the end of the age" (Matt 28, 18–20).

3. Brief Exegesis

This text of "the commissioning of the disciples" as has been documented by Mathew (Matt 28,16–20), plays three major concluding roles in the entire gospel: It concludes and brings to a climax the resurrection narrative of Matt 28,1–20, the passion-resurrection narrative of Matt 26,1–28,20, and the entire Gospel.[5] The emphasis of the whole text is found in the last three verses, vv. 18–20. This emphasis is brought out firstly by the serious implications of the very words used by Jesus in the commissioning and, secondly, by their grammatical and syntactical arrangement.

Thus, that Jesus himself "came to them" (*proselthon*) shows a comforting approach by the risen Lord as he takes the initiative to re-establish an intimate relationship with the disciples after his resurrection from the dead.[6] This approach also sees Jesus going further to reassure the disciples regarding what he is about to do by making reference to his comprehensive authority: "all authority in heaven and on earth has been given to me" (Matt 28,18). Jesus' use of the passive verb (*edothe moi – is given*) presupposes God as the subject. Hence, it is God himself who has given him this comprehensive authority over the whole of the created order. Of course, during his earthly ministry, before his death and resurrection, Jesus made serious references to this authority that he has. Hence, in 9,6, he refers to his "authority on earth to forgive sins." In 11,27, he declares authorita-

---

4 SENIOR, 344.
5 D. A. HAGNER, *Matthew 14–28* (Word Biblical Commentary, 33B; Dallas: Word Books, 1995) 881.
6 HAGNER, *Matthew 14–28*, 886.

tively: "all things have been handed over to me by my Father." Therefore, by beginning this "commissioning" this way, Jesus strongly reassures his disciples, as the resurrection has clearly vindicated his words and deeds during his earthly ministry. It is indeed "God's validation" of everything that he did and taught.[7] Consequently, it is this glorified Jesus, who has the sovereign authority of God, who now sends out his disciples on this mission to evangelise the whole world, thus providing them the needed authority and confidence for that serious task.[8]

The evangelist presents Jesus' commission by means of one central imperative verb, "make disciples," (*matheteusate*) which is accompanied by three syntactically subordinate participles, "going" (*poreuthentes*), "baptising" (*baptizontes*), and "teaching" (*didaskontes*). Grammatically, though, these participles take on the force of the imperative because the main verb is in the imperative mood.[9] The subject of the main verb is "all nations" (*panta ta ethne*). Therefore, the disciples are to go into the whole world and evangelise it and make disciples for Jesus from all corners of the earth. They are to baptise them in the name of the Trinity. Also, they are to teach these disciples to observe all that Jesus has commanded them. This instruction to baptise the future disciples and to teach them to observe all that Jesus has commanded, strongly indicates that these commissioned disciples are not just going to make new future disciples. That is only the first step. They should also further incorporate them into the community through baptism, through "a discipling-and-teaching process that must continue indefinitely."[10]

One thing becomes very clear from our text, especially considering its grammatical, syntactical, and general philological arrangement. That thing is this: It is the universal authority of Jesus, which is the basis of the universal mission of his disciples and the Church. This is crystal clear from the text we are considering. To that end, after Jesus asserts his universal authority in

---

7 T. G. LONG, *Matthew* (Westminster Bible Companion; Louisville: Westminster John Knox, 1997) 325.
8 HAGNER, *Matthew 14–28*, 886.
9 HAGNER, *Matthew 14 – 28*, 886.
10 D. R. A. HARE, *Matthew* (Interpretation; Louisville: John Knox Press, 1993) 334.

v.18, the evangelist introduces his command to his disciples to go and make disciples of all nations by using the connecting word "therefore" (*oun*) that shows "consequence." Furthermore, to end the instructions, Jesus again promises his disciples his abiding presence with them to the end of time (v. 20). The evangelist calls attention to the special character of this last promise by using the particle "look" or "remember" (*idou*). Thus, "Jesus' authority (v. 18) and his presence (v. 20) will empower his disciples to fulfil the commission he now gives them."[11]

All that has been explained so far highlights this commissioning of the disciples by Jesus as a very serious matter. The evangelist has presented it as such both through his language and the arrangement of that language. Consequently, at the end of this gospel, very pertinent issues attract a new impetus following from the authority and abiding presence of the risen Lord with his disciples. For the first time, the confinement of the gospel to Israel (10,5; 15,24) is removed. The gospel is now to be preached to all nations, as is already anticipated in 24,14; 26,13 – and this task has been noted and taken seriously right from the early Church (Mark 16,15; acts 1,8; Col 1,23), as has already been said. The Gentiles are now fully included in salvation history as the evangelist has already hinted in the stories of the Magi (2, 1–12), the centurion (8,5–13) and the Canaanite woman's daughter (15,21–28). This is also the fulfilment of the promise which God had made to Abraham many years ago in the OT, because he (Abraham) had obeyed God: "…and by your offspring shall all the nations of the earth gain blessing for themselves, because you have obeyed my voice" (Gen 22, 18). Furthermore, the promise of Jesus, "I am with you," v. 20, recall the text of 18, 20 where he promises to be among two or three "gathered in my name." It also echoes in a special way the identification of Jesus as Emmanuel, "God with us," at the very beginning of the gospel (Matt 1, 23). These connections bring out clearly the unity of the gospel of Matthew that they enclose in a wonderful *inclusio*,[12] hinged on the abiding presence of Jesus with his disciples. Also, this promise echoes many OT passages that

---

11 HAGNER, *Matthew 14 – 28*, 886.
12 W. D. DAVIES – D. C. ALLISON, Jr., *The Gospel According to Saint Matthew*, Vol. III (A Critical and Exegetical Commentary; Edinburgh: T & T. Clark, 1997) 688.

promise God's presence with his people. For example, God had assured Jacob: "Know that I am with you and will keep you wherever you go, and will bring you back to this land; for I will not leave you until I have done what I have promised you" (Gen 28,15; cf. also Hag 1,13; Exod 3,12; Isa 41,10). Hence: "Where Yahweh was formally with his people, Jesus is now with his people, the Church. Jesus, though not physically present among them, will not have abandoned them. He will be in their midst, though unseen, and will empower them to fulfil the commission he has given them. Those who receive the messengers of the good news will receive Jesus himself (10, 40). And the promise of Jesus' continuing presence with them is not restricted to any special circumstances (but includes persecution as well as ministry), nor is it made simply for the immediate future. He will be with them... 'all the days until the consummation of the age.'"[13]

Therefore, at the end of the gospel, the evangelist arrives at an admirable unity of the entire gospel by ending the whole account with the story of this commissioning of his disciples by the risen Lord and his promise of remaining with them always (Matt 28, 16–20). And by reporting, at that juncture, Jesus' emphasis that the disciples have the duty to go and make disciples of all the nations, the evangelist also succeeds in setting up an involving program of action for the post resurrection community of Jesus' followers – the Church – thereby ensuring its continuity with the ministry of the earthly Jesus himself. It is a program that really "looks forward to the continuing work of the Messianic Community."[14] It is this program, then, which has seen the Church spread virtually to all the corners of the earth, including our country, Nigeria.

4. Application

All things considered, therefore, one has to say that immense thanks must always be given to God regarding the development of the Church and its role in the whole world. All through history, the Church has been a major force to be reckoned with in all aspects of development in our world. In her

---

13 HAGNER, *Matthew 14 – 28*, 888–889.
14 W. F. ALBRIGHT – C. S. MANN, *Matthew* (The Anchor Bible 26; New York: Doubleday & Co, 1971) 361.

quest to preach the gospel to the whole world, the Church has also seriously helped to foster peace, justice, and equality among all peoples.

Coming back home, one must never fail to give God immense thanks for his many blessings to our country, Nigeria. The Church keeps playing very laudable roles in all the aspects of our life, national, state, local government, and at the level of the individual. In many parts of the country, Christians have also helped to shape the polity with the result that we are gradually witnessing increased responsiveness and responsibility on the part of government.

Above all, the Church in Nigeria, particularly in Igbo land, has been blessed with an active laity and abundant vocations to the priesthood and the religious life. Granted that all that glitters may not be gold, and this axiom, of course, applies equally to the human situation all over the world, yet it is completely in order to keep thanking and praising God for his immense love for us and all our people which is especially manifested in the gift of our local and universal Church. It would then always be our constant duty, in the light of our Lord's commission of his disciples, to endeavour to always properly watch over the flock that has been entrusted to us (1 Peter 5,1–4).

It is especially on this note that I am personally thanking God for the rare gift of PD Akpunonu to us in the Church. He has really contributed immensely to the welfare, growth, and sustenance of the Church both locally and internationally. For this task, he was really well prepared.

PD Akpunonu studied theology in Rome at the Urban University (1962–1966). He studied Sacred Scripture at the Pontifical Biblical Institute (Biblicum), also in Rome (1967–1970). He got his doctorate at the Urban University, Rome, after serious studies both at Jerusalem and Rome (1970–1971).

After all those long years of studies which have been shown above, PD Akpunonu returned to Nigeria and was immediately saddled with the task of forming future priests. Hence, he became a formator at Bigard Memorial Seminary, Enugu (1972–1978) and substantive rector at Bigard from 1979 to 1989. From 1989–1997, PD Akpunonu was the rector of "The Catholic Institute of West Africa" (CIWA), Port Harcourt. He taught at Mundelein University in the United States of America (1997–2013) and also helped out in teaching senior seminarians there. It was also during this sojourn at the United States that he bagged his professorship. In 2013, he finally returned to Nigeria after many years abroad. His main aim for coming back to his fatherland is principally to contribute, as much as he still can, in the spreading of the gospel, especially in the formation of future priests. Since his return, he has been helping out in the formation of our seminarians, especially at Blessed Iwene Tansi Major Seminary, Onitsha.

All the seminarians who have had the privilege of attending the lectures and conferences given by PD, as he is fondly called, as well as the Masses regularly celebrated by him at Blessed Iwene Tansi Major Seminary, have never ceased to thank God for those highly enriching opportunities. Even some of our young priests have taken time to note the periods for his lectures in the seminary class timetable. They have been attending those lectures from their different parishes and places of assignment!

5. Personal Reflection and Conclusion

I came to know PD as my rector at Bigard Memorial Seminary, Enugu, from 1985 to 1989. In fact, we were the last group of students trained completely by him at Bigard. I was particularly close to him in the area of music, as I then functioned as the seminary main organist for almost four years. Later, after I had been ordained a priest, I also stayed with him at CIWA, Port Harcourt, during the 1994/95 academic year before travelling abroad to continue my studies. I consider it not necessary to make a litany of PD's sterling qualities. Suffice it to say that PD is, indeed, a rare gem, an invaluable gift to the local and universal Church. Even at unbelievably and unimaginably difficult times, PD remains a shining example for all, especially for priests and religious people.

In short, PD has struggled, in his entire life, to carry out that commission of Jesus to his disciples, as it is recorded by Matthew the Evangelist: "Go therefore and make disciples of all nations, baptising them in the name of the Father and of the Son and of the Holy Spirit, and teaching them to obey everything that I have commanded you. And remember, I am with you always, to the end of the age" (Matt 28,18–20) – and it is this "commission" that we have been dwelling upon in this article.

As PD celebrates the golden jubilee of his priestly ordination, I join his numerous friends, well wishers, admirers and students in praying for him, thanking God for him and wishing him God's choicest blessings and many more years of fruitful service in the Lord's vineyard. More grease to your elbows, our dearly beloved PD!!!

References

D. A. HAGNER, *Matthew 14–28*, Word Biblical Commentary, 33B; Dallas: Word Books, 1995.

D. R. A. HARE, *Matthew* Interpretation; Louisville: John Knox Press, 1993.

D. SENIOR, *Matthew* Abingdon New Testament Commentaries; Nashville: Abingdon Press, 1998.

T. G. LONG, *Matthew* Westminster Bible Companion; Louisville: Westminster John Knox, 1997.

W. D. DAVIES – D. C. ALLISON, Jr., *The Gospel According to Saint Matthew*, Vol. III, A Critical and Exegetical Commentary; Edinburgh: T & T. Clark, 1997.

W. F. ALBRIGHT – C. S. MANN, *Matthew* The Anchor Bible 26; New York: Doubleday & Co, 1971.

Martin Joe U. Ibeh

Gaudium et spes at 50: Integrating Social Mission into the Centre of Catholic Life in Nigeria

1. Introduction

For many reasons, the year 2015 is a special year in the life of the Catholic Church. Exactly fifty years ago, the Church celebrated the end of the Second Vatican Council. No other event in the 20th century has shaken and shaped the Church in its structure, self-understanding, belief, and practice as well as its relationship to the outside world as Vatican II. Celebrating its golden jubilee is appropriate and necessary not only from the point of view of its historical importance but also from the point of view of the themes debated during the sessions as well as the documents produced.

Two of the most outstanding documents of the Council were *Lumen gentium* and *Gaudium et spes*. While Lumen gentium (dogmatic constitution on the Church) addressed the internal nature and life of the Church, Gaudium et spes focused on the Church's relationship to the modern world. Before Vatican II, the Church was conducting a self-maintenance operation. It needed a re-definition that included its task in the world. The main focus of this limited paper is to highlight the centrality of this dialogue with the modern world, to sketch the heart of Catholic social teaching, and to underline social ministry as an integral part of the Church's life and witness in Nigeria.

The golden jubilee of Vatican II is a special event for all Catholics, for a few individuals, it's also a double celebration. Very Rev. Fr. Dr. Peter Damian Akpunonu celebrates in January 2016 his priestly golden jubilee. As a theology student of the renowned Pontifical Urban University, Rome, he had the rare privilege of observing and experiencing the Council, and witnessing the promulgation of its documents. Pope Paul VI (a Council Father) promulgated *Gaudium et spes* on 7th December 1965, four weeks

later, he ordained Peter Damian a Catholic priest. This paper is a humble
contribution to the celebration of both historical events.

2. Background and Central Message of *Gaudium et spes*[1]

In a genuinely significant manner the Pastoral Constitution on the Church in
the modern world – *Gaudium et spes* – set out to redefine the Church. It was
"the longest document of the Council, indeed the longest document ever
produced by any of the 21 ecumenical Councils in a 2,000 year history."[2]
The opening words of the great document read:

> "The joys and the hopes, the griefs and the anxieties of the men of this age, es-
> pecially those who are poor or in any way afflicted, these are the joys and hopes,
> the griefs and anxieties of the followers of Christ. ... That is why this community
> realizes that it is truly linked with mankind and its history by the deepest of
> bonds" (GS 1).

Gaudium et spes, often referred to as "the great document," was not
planned from the outset of the Council. Three Cardinals championed its
cause: Belgian Cardinal Leo Suenes, Cardinal Giovanni Battista Montini
of Milan (later Pope Paul VI), and Cardinal Lercaro of Bologna. These
and other Council Fathers had experienced the trauma of two world wars,
the Holocaust, nuclear weaponry, communism, and the cold war. These
experiences informed their sense of urgency to get the Church to focus on
a new model of Church/world engagement. This is because "previous models were no longer adequate: the minority sect within the Roman empire,
the alliance of Church and Constantinian state, the medieval institution
of Christendom, the battered and battering Church of post-Reformation
Europe, the established Church of the ancien regime, and the isolated and
triumphalistic Church of the 19th century."[3]

   A non-internal definition of the Church has to address the issue of Christian eschatology and worldly progress, responsibility for the society of

---

1   This section of the paper relies extensively on Thomas Rosica's recent analysis
    of *Gaudium et spes* as it turns 50.
2   Thomas Rosica, *"Gaudium et Spes at 50": A keynote address delivered to the
    Association of United States Catholic Priests in St. Louis, Missouri on June 30th*,
    2015, accessed from: http://www.zenit.org/.
3   Thomas Rosica (2015).

tomorrow, the responsibility of Christians, and Christian ethics. The final result was the Pastoral Constitution on the Church in the modern world. With its promulgation, the Council signalled its intention and mission to evangelise, to share the good news of salvation via a new method. It dealt with many issues: political and economic issues, the challenge of contemporary atheism, the inviolability of human dignity, the dignity and holiness of marriage and family life, individualistic culture that lacks ethical anchor and confuses the true meaning of love between spouses, destructive fury of war, and terrorism. Consequently, *"Gaudium et spes* suggested a Church with a new strategy for the Church's presence in the world, one which emphasised neither withdrawal, triumphalism, nor assimilation, but critical conversation (listening and speaking) along with principled cooperation with other social institutions and communities of people. The mission of the Church needed to be expressed in social categories and had, therefore, to take seriously the realities of secularization and pluralism."[4]

The main features of this document leaned on both encyclicals of Pope John XXIII namely *Mater er Magistra* (1961) and *Pacem in terris* (1963). It is divided into two major parts. After the presentation of the basic anthropology of Christian humanism in chapters one through three, chapters eleven to forty-five dealt with general issues concerning the Church and the call of man, and chapters forty-six to ninety treated other individual issues. In a summary, the entire document considered the Church's contribution in building a world that acknowledges and promotes the dignity, life and freedom of each human person; the creation of conditions of justice and peace for individuals and communities; active participation of the Church in the international community; Church's neutrality with regard to political, economic or social systems; and the establishment and consolidation of peace in the world as a human family. As the "oldest global player,"[5] the Catholic Church is structurally more advanced in human cooperation and can provide an example of how different continents, nations and cultures can work together without losing their individual identities.

---

4   Thomas Rosica (2015).
5   Cf. Joachim Wiemeyer, Keine Freiheit ohne Gerechtigkeit. Christliche Sozialethik angesichts globaler Herausforderungen, Herder Verlag, Freiburg im Breisgau 2015.

In re-conceptualizing its mission, therefore, the Church has the task of always "scrutinizing the signs of the times and of interpreting them in the light of the Gospel. …We must therefore recognize and understand the world in which we live, its expectations, its longings, its often dramatic characteristics."[6] Another document which responded in a more synthetic and more concrete way to the challenges of the times was the declaration *Nostra aetate*.

3. The Heart of Catholic Social Teaching

Catholic social teaching evolved from the reaction to social issues that characterised the 19th century.[7] Never in the two thousand-year history of the Church had any ecumenical Council taken the stride to delve into the temporal events of humanity with such pastoral profundity. Two documents dealt specifically with social issues: *Dignitatis humanae* (on religious freedom) and *Gaudium et spes* (on the Church in the modern world).[8] *Gaudium et spes* did not invent the Church's social teaching, it rather it drew insights from it: "In the course of the centuries," the Church "has worked out, in the light of the Gospel, principles of justice and equity demanded by right reason for individual and social life and also for international relations. The Council now intends to reiterate those principles in accordance with the situation in the world today and will outline certain guidelines" (GS 63). As Roger Charles SJ noted, Gaudium et spes "was broader in scope than the individual social encyclicals, concerned as they were with responding to specific social issues or situations."[9]

So, *Gaudium et spes* confronted theologically the fundamental questions that have always plagued the human heart, defining the Church in terms of its task in the world. With this pastoral constitution, the Council Fathers contributed in a most significant manner in the formulation and development of Catholic social teaching: "*Gaudium et spes* was extraordinary as a document because it gave a coherent picture of Catholic social teaching. But it goes even

---

6   Thomas Rosica (2015).
7   Cf. Joachim Wiemeyer (2015).
8   Roger Charles SJ, Christian Social Witness and Teaching, Cromwell Press, Wiltshire 1998.
9   Roger Charles SJ (1998).

further than that. It gives a new and coherent picture of what is essential to being a Christian, what is essential to being Church in the world."[10]

At the heart of Catholic social teaching is social justice. Justice has been referred to as the supreme form of virtue, that virtue which is closest to the "divine mind." Its proper act, according to Aquinas, "is nothing else than to render to each one what is their own," *their own* being "that which is due to them according to equality of proportion." Justice entails the idea of equality, that each person is a reflection of the divine image and should receive according to their due. Injustice is that state in which "one attributes to oneself too many of the benefits and too few of the burdens."[11]

There are three classical aspects of justice: *Legal justice (justitia legalis)* concerns what the citizen owes in fairness to the community.[12] Included are individuals, groups, organizations and even the state. The denial of the essential goods that are necessary for someone to maintain a family, for example, contravenes this principle. *Commutative justice (justitia commutativa)* regulates the relationship between individual members and groups within and among themselves. *Distributive justice (iustitia distributiva)* refers to the patristic notion that material goods beyond what is needed for living with dignity are owed to the community so that all may live in dignity. *Contributive justice (justitia contributiva),* according to Arno Anzenbacher,[13] is that aspect of justice which guarantees citizens active participation, in freedom and dignity, in the life of the society. In his view, all these four distinctions come under the umbrella of social justice, and social justice itself is at the service of the common good.[14]

Social justice as an integral part of Catholic social teaching "is based on the rights that flow from and safeguard human dignity, and it compels us to work with others to help make social institutions better serve the common

10 Thomas Rosica (2015).
11 Martin Joe U. Ibeh, Environmental Ethics and Politics in the Developing Countries. A Case Study from Nigeria, Schöningh Verlag Paderborn, 2002.
12 *Catechism of the Catholic Church,* Geoffrey Chapman, London, 1994. Nr. 2411.
13 Arno Anzenbacher, Christliche Sozialethik: Einführung und Prinzipien, Schöningh Verlag Paderborn, 1998.
14 Reinhard Marx & Helge Wulsdorf, Christliche Sozialethik: Konturen – Prinzipien – Handlungsfelder, AMATECA Lehrbücher zur katholischen Theologie, Band XXI, Bonifatius GmbH Verlag Paderborn, 2002.

good."[15] The Catechism of the Catholic Church (especially 1928–1948) and the Compendium of the Social Doctrine of the Church (published in 2004) both present a magnificent overview of the wider topic of the Church's social doctrine and social justice.

The importance of formulating a concept of justice that recognises the classical aspects of justice is inalienable, but at the same time, this concept must address the complexity of modern society. To achieve this objective, Catholic social teaching has a lot to contribute in its fruitful dialogue with areas of life; such as, economics, politics, ethics, art, social relations, etc. In contemporary politics, words like "left" or "right," "liberal" or "conservative" are used to describe ideological concepts.[16] Catholic social teaching is neither of these. As a moral and ethical enterprise, it is not content with statements on social issues, but sets moral accent on individual concrete situations and proffers practical suggestions. It does so – without presuming to provide answer to every given situation – based on the fundamental ethical principles it stands for in such areas as social justice, equality, freedom, sustainability, solidarity, subsidiarity, etc.

Social teachings of the Church especially on justice and peace, together with pastoral letters of bishops, need to be more effectively communicated to the grass-roots of the local Church. Catholic institutions like seminaries, theological institutes, novitiates, catechetical centres, schools, etc., provide veritable platforms to do so. Appropriate methods should be developed and tried. In this way, the people of God will become familiar with the Church's documents and messages. The first Catholic bishop of Awka, Albert K. Obiefuna, introduced diocesan quizzes for schools based on his pastoral letters. It was an exercise that made impact.

4. Social Ministry as an Integral Part of the Life and Mission of the Church in Nigeria

The work of the Second Vatican Council, the central message and challenge of *Gaudium et spes* is not over. Nigeria is part of the global Church. As we celebrate with all Catholics this golden jubilee, we need to integrate social

---

15 Thomas Rosica (2015).
16 Thomas Rosica (2015).

mission into the centre of our Catholic life. We must proclaim the social gospel fully and vividly. We must insist that social ministry is an integral part of the life and mission of the Church in this part of the world. In the words of *Thomas Rosica*, "we can no longer speak of 'social justice' as an option or an alternative. Our incorporation and implementation of the social teaching of the Church must become normative and constitutive."[17] We must renew and strengthen our sense of mission in many areas.

4.1 Nigerian Societal Paradox

Nigeria is one of the largest oil and gas exporting nations in the world. However, the life-situation of Nigerians as a people is that of economic poverty and dependency in the midst of plenty and wealth. There is this general disappointment, especially among young people, that the government has failed to fight poverty and create wealth und sustainable development. A World Bank Economic Report from 2014 estimated that the national per capita poverty rate remained very high at more than 60% of the population, with little evidence of recent progress in poverty reduction. The urban measurement stood at 12.6%, while in the rural areas it was 44.9%. The poverty line used was N180 per day, which was equivalent to about $1.25 per day at the purchasing power parity (PPP). With an estimated GDP of $509 billion, making Nigeria the 26th largest economy in the world, how could a country of the size and wealth of Nigeria have poverty rates much higher than in surrounding countries like Niger and Benin Republic, the report asks.[18] That is the paradox.

In the eighties and nineties, the corrupt and incompetent elite clinched unto power, enriched themselves, and forgot the masses. This trend continued. One observes increasing division and gaps between the super rich and super poor, the super powerful and super powerless, the propertied and non-propertied, the job-holders and jobless, the well-educated and illiterates, the frequent flyers and village champions, etc. A minority of Nigeria's population has the greatest proportion of the wealth. Lack of adequate infrastructure that includes good road networks, permanent power supply,

---

17 Thomas Rosica (2015).
18 Accessed from: http://www.worldbank.org/.

affordable portable water and health insurance – all make life in the cities and suburbs unbearable. The scourge of AIDS, prostitution and the trafficking of women and children, the decline in moral values, fuelled by the trivialisation of sexuality in the media and entertainment industries – all lead to the degradation of women and even the abuse of children. The complexity of this unspeakable human exploitation demands a concerted national response.

The superiority of politics to competence in the Nigerian leadership is a major problem. The principle of quota system, even with its advantages, promotes mediocrity and incompetence; in the name of regional and ethnic considerations, excellence and productivity are relegated to the background, especially in such areas as education and public service. Corruption is a recurrent decimal and household attribute; it has permeated every aspect of political and social life. The Corruption Perceptions Index conducted by Transparency International annually ranks countries and territories based on how corrupt their public sector is perceived to be. According to 2014 Index, Nigeria ranked 136 out of 175 countries and territories. Again, a country's score indicates the perceived level of public sector corruption on a scale of 0 (highly corrupt) to 100 (very clean); here Nigeria scored 27.[19] Of course, external factors like debt burden, structural adjustment programs, austerity measures and incessant conflicts have aggravated the situation. Again, neo-liberalism floated by the World Bank and International Monetary Fund as alternative ideology did create an economic boom, however, it benefited only the upper class. Even the western model of education, for many reasons, has failed to achieve breakthroughs in the areas of development and innovation.

The demographic development of the country is a cause for concern. The recent population report of the United Nations predicts that by the year 2050, Nigeria with approximately 399 million inhabitants would be the third largest country in the world, after China and India.[20] Our leaders do not seem to hear the warning bell. The brain drain that began in the eighties through nineties has not stopped. Nigerian top IT-experts, for example, work and create fortunes overseas. Thousands of "economic" and

---

19 Accessed from: http://www.transparency.org/.
20 Accessed from: http://www.un.org/en/index.shtml.

political refugees abandon the country by air, through the Sahara desert, or by boats in search of greener pasture in Europe, America, Asia, and even in other African countries like Angola and South Africa. The number of Nigerians that have drowned inside the Mediterranean Sea or perished in the deserts over the past years is anybody's guess. Many who made it are now stranded; some end up as drug traffickers, criminals, or perpetual beggars. Nigeria has no good name overseas; every Nigerian is a suspect, you have to prove beyond reasonable doubts that you are not like them. Among those who stay back are thousands of graduates and those half-educated without jobs and professional know-how; they flood the streets of our major cities like Abuja, Lagos or Onitsha in search of opportunities to better their financial base.

All these awry developments provide a veritable ground for radical movements within the country itself. Young men, who think globalisation has turned them into losers, easily fall prey to political, ethnic, or religious manipulation. They are so disappointed that they no longer believe politicians, including the call of religious leaders for tolerance, dialogue, and renounce of violence. A little amount of money is enough to sway and enslave them. The incessant acts of robbery and kidnapping have reached astronomical dimensions, and the law-enforcement agencies of the land have done little to stem the tide.

Millions of people leave unexpectedly their traditional contexts and confront themselves with new ideas, values, and lifestyles. The feeling of losing one's identity leads to a flight back to original convictions. Traditional churches are witnessing a mass exodus of members especially from the younger generation; they seek new spiritual community among the evangelicals and charismatic movements, and others are deeply rooted in occultism and neo-paganism. Most problematic, according to Wolfgang Schonecke,[21] are the radical churches – crusaders and evangelists – from America, Europe, and other African countries. Through promises of healings, exorcism, and wealth creation, they attract thousands of people to their fold. The German evangelist Reinhard Bonnke, for example, campaigned heavily once

---

21 Cf. Wolfgang Schonecke, „Hat Toleranz noch eine Chance? Bedrohungen des christlich-islamischen Dialogs in Afrika," in: Herder Korrespondenz, Heft 6, Juni 2014.

in the city of Kano in northern Nigeria in 1991. It led to serious conflicts that cost hundreds of lives. The same is true of the different radical Islamic movements. Their political ideologies and movements are gaining more and more influence. Propelled by their Saudi Arabian and Egyptian connections and affiliations with Al-Kaida groups, their aim is simply the eradication of syncretistic tendencies in Islam. They strive by all means to convert all Moslems to true believers of Islam. Hugely financed with petrodollars, they are able to build mosques, establish schools and universities, and train Imams and preachers in order to propagate their new ideas. In predominantly Muslim areas, these fundamentalists demand the recognition of Islam as the State religion and the introduction of the Sharia. This becomes a reality where the democratic process allows it. Radical salafists engage in violence where this is not the case. The Nigerian Boko Haram is a typical example of how religious fanaticism can end up in terrorism. No serious foreign investor can dare such a social, economic, and political climate.

Looking at this despicable picture of Nigeria, the Church cannot just keep quiet. It has a huge stake in the affairs of the land, because what touches the citizens touches its members. The Church needs to raise its voice and get into dialogue with our leaders. Nigeria needs fresh blood and new ideas. What is important is an end to political instability and poor policy implementation. There is a need to restructure the national economic order in a way and manner that helps to bridge the wide gap between the wealthy and poor so that all and every child of God will have a fair share in earthly goods. The wealthy should be made to pay more tax and be encouraged to invest their money in enterprises that create more jobs.[22] Nigeria can no longer depend only on oil and gas; new nations have joined the league of oil and gas producers. The volatile market prices in this sector have forced the government to review its annual budgets. We have other latent resources that need to be discovered and developed. The agricultural sector, for instance, needs urgent and decisive attention. Equally vital is an end to inefficient use of resources, so that a more effective distribution could create jobs. Government should do more in tackling inadequate infrastructure in the cities and suburbs. The new government should distinguish itself by

---

22 Cf. Lucius I. Ugorji, The Memoirs of a Shepherd on Social Problems and Theological Themes of the Day, Snaap Press Ltd., Enugu, 2000.

targeting economic growth, providing skill-training and jobs for millions of young people, educating women and girls for life, overcoming the endemic cancer of corruption, guaranteeing freedom of movement and speech, and adequate security. Furthermore, everyone who plays a role in public life and those who participate in governing the country should do everything in their power to restore hope to the people, so that everyone may benefit from the profits of the natural and economic resources, in accordance with the principles of justice and equity. Like everyone else, the poor have the right to justice, decent work, adequate food, health and education, in accordance with the Universal Declaration of Human Rights, as well as other rights found in other international instruments. The demand for social justice is not only made on individual persons but above all, on the state and just institutions for a just order in society. With this in mind, the state should establish laws and norms that will facilitate the achievement of this social justice. Principal elements of this social justice include commutative justice, legal justice, distributive and contributive justice.[23]

4.2 Prophetic Voice in Society

As already mentioned, what is required of the Church is a prophetic voice that will capture the imagination of the world. Evangelisation in Nigeria necessarily includes the praxis of the Gospel and active commitment to liberate humanity from poverty, suffering and oppression. These are the demands of the social Gospel. This was the example of Jesus and it is the inescapable duty of the Church. The Church's effort to fulfil its prophetic mission in society has often been met with strong opposition even from among Christians on the ground that it is interfering in political affairs; the Church should concern itself more with the spiritual well-being of believers. The Church argues that since solidarity and justice belong to the core of biblical and Christian ethics, it has a message/gospel for all men and women. The Church commits itself to the value of solidarity and justice as a decisive benchmark for a future-oriented and sustainable economic and social politics.[24] In fulfilling its obligation, the Church recognises its limits.

---

23 Cf. Martin Joe U. Ibeh (2003).
24 Cf. Martin Joe U. Ibeh (2003).

It is neither a referee nor has it all the answers. Its mission is to pursue whatever cause that serves equality and the common good. This involves calling for good management of economic and public affairs, enabling the people to see politics as a service of God and seeking the route of a good democratic government.[25]

It is for the Church in Nigeria to chart effective ways of fulfilling her task of societal transformation and liberation of the people from their life-situation. Ways for achieving societal transformation and more equitable social order in Nigeria include taking part in the political education of the masses; electing morally upright and knowledgeable people to political offices; helping directly or indirectly to change bad or inefficient government; taking moral or Christian education of the young seriously. As Barnabas C.Okolo[26] rightly argued, in electing a morally upright and knowledgeable people to political offices, religious affiliation must play a secondary role. A good Moslem is better than a corrupt Christian.

In the past, the Church had failed to mobilise the faithful to take up their civic responsibility of being actively involved in politics. Presently, the people of God especially east of the Niger are being involved in democratic education and political life. They are throwing themselves more and more wholeheartedly or unequivocally into the struggle for better conditions, or for the upholding of human rights. The recent return of schools in Anambra State taken over in the seventies from the churches is a landmark for posterity. The fruits are becoming evident. Since then, for example, the educational performance of the State is unequalled throughout the Federation.

However vulnerable the Church might be, in order not to compromise its mission as leaven of society, the Church must avoid becoming identified with oppressive political structures and regimes. The Church should exert pressure for a greater measure of cooperation between north and south,

---

25 Cf. Communiqué of Seminar organized by the Episcopal Commission for Justice, Development and Peace of the Catholic Bishops' Conference of Nigeria (CBCN), Jos, 1996.
26 Barnabas C.Okolo, Social Teachings in *Gaudium et spes:* The Nigerian Connection, in: Obiora F. Ike, ed., Catholic Social Teachings En-Route in Africa, Snaap Press Ltd., Enugu, 1991.

east and west, and encourage Nigerians to set their own agenda for the recovery and development of the country.

4.3 Church of the Poor for the Poor[27]

The horizontal and vertical dimensions of the gospel are at the heart of evangelisation and liberation theology. Holiness cannot flourish in sub-human conditions. The whole purpose of liberation theology is the fight against sin and selfishness, which are the root causes of social injustice and exploitation of both man and resources. One of the subtle but prophetic voices during the Council, according to Michael Sievernich,[28] was the Arch-bishop Dom Hélder Câmara Pessoa (1909–1999) of Olinda e Recife in the poor North-East of Brazil. He never delivered any speech but through his power of communication among his fellow bishops and connection to the media he became one of the major figures of the Council. He was a member of various Council commissions and informal conferences and groups. He became the voice of the voiceless poor within the group that handled the topic "Church of the poor."

Thanks to such efforts, it was possible to anchor the issue of poverty in some of the texts of the Council. In both pastoral Constitution texts, the poor were considered as the theological locus where the Church recognises the picture of its founder, who himself knew poverty and suffering (LG 8). With this insight the mission is clear: Christ in the poor is calling his disciples to action (GS 88). An American lay observer James J. Norris had the opportunity to deliver a powerful paper on poverty in the world. Issues concerning poverty and international development cooperation were taken up in the texts dealing on building an international community (GS 83–90) and also inspired in practical ways the establishment of Church aid organizations.

Soon after the Council, as Michael Sievernich reported, Archbishop Dom Hélder Câmara Pessoa tried in various ways, especially through

---

27 A lot of information on this was taken from Michael Sievernich's recent assessment of Vatican II.

28 Michael Sievernich, Erst die Ouvertüre. Das Zweite Vatikanum als Konzil der Weltkirche? in: Herder Korrespondenz Spezial, Konzil im Konflikt, 50 Jahre Zweites Vatikanum, Oktober 2012 .

publications, to implement the reforms of the Council in his diocese and also in the whole of Latin American Church. The conferences of Medelín (1968) and Puebla (1969) the Latin American Episcopal Council (CELAM) dealt with the essential impulses of the Council and subsequent social encyclical "*Populorum progressio*"; they came up with the "preferential option for the poor" that has become one of the basic principles of Catholic social teaching of the 20th century. The Compendium of the Social Doctrine of the Church[29] categorically states: "The principle of the universal destination of goods requires that the poor, the marginalized and in all cases those whose living conditions interfere with their proper growth should be the focus of particular concern. To this end, the preferential option for the poor should be reaffirmed in all its force." Furthermore, "This is an option, or a *special form* of primacy in the exercise of Christian charity, to which the whole tradition of the Church bears witness... given the worldwide dimension which the social question has assumed, this love of preference for the poor, and the decisions which it inspires in us, cannot but embrace the immense multitudes of the hungry, the needy, the homeless, those without health care and, above all, those without hope of a better future"[384–385].

The task of the Church consists in championing the cause of liberating the people and society. This liberative act is integrally connected with and solidly based on the principles of justice, peace, and development. God's liberative act in the history of his chosen ones[30] provides the Church in Nigeria the impetus and obligation to be on the path of liberation for the people. Since the poor are many times, by their very condition, excluded from society, their capacity to secure their rights is often very limited. That is why the Church must put the eradication of poverty at the heart of evangelisation as well as social agendas.

Pope Paul VI performed some symbolical acts in this direction. With the removal of the papal Triple Crown and its power symbolism on 13th of November 1964, he placed himself on the forefront of the march to defend and care for the poor. Another landmark was his travels to India (1964),

---

29 *Compendium of the Social Doctrine of the Church*, Libreria Editrice Vaticana 2004.

30 "I have seen the affliction of my people and have heard their cry ... I know their suffering." Exodus 3:7

Colombia (1968), and Uganda (1969). Dozens of bishops followed suit with the famous "Catacomb pact" in the Domitilla-Catacomb where they pledged to draw attention to poverty in the Church through renunciation of title and power, and pursue social justice through a simple lifestyle.[31]

The Nigerian Church has to be on the side of the poor too. Their cries against injustice, exploitation, power play, poverty, and artificial inflation have become unbearable. Jesus himself challenged existing structures both religious and political and got into trouble and paid a price for it with his life. In imitation of their master, bishops, priests, religious, the faithful, and all men and women of goodwill are enjoined to "champion the cause of the poor and fight injustice at private, social and institutional levels of our society."[32] There are three ways of helping the poor. First of all, they need material help in form of money and other essential needs like food, housing, clothing, hospital bill, education, etc. This is solidarity. Secondly, one can show solidarity by joining them in their struggle against personal and individual sins as well as social sins, institutionalised or located in socio-political structures. The third form of help is to live poor; it means human touch, embracing, sharing, simplicity of life, and a new logic.

The first Latin American Pope, Francis, emphasises these forms of solidarity. In his young papacy, he has left both critics and admirers in no doubt about how he perceives his call as "the servant of the servants of men." He preaches mercy and calls on all Catholics to be merciful. He has a passion for the poor, the immigrant, the forgotten, and the marginalised. Thomas Rosica describes him as: "Pope Francis is becoming for us the activation or embodiment of pastoral constitution on the Church in the World. ... He has not changed a single doctrine of the Church but has ushered in a way of speaking, a new style of leadership that has shaken the Church and impacted the world."[33] Reacting to the issue of the surge of migrants, Pope Francis urges Europe and America to welcome refugees. More concretely, he called on every parish, every religious institution, and every monastery to welcome a family: "When I talk about a parish welcoming a family, I do not mean that they should go and live in the parish house, but rather that

---

31 Michael Sievernich (2012).
32 cf. Communiqué, CBCN (1996).
33 Thomas Rosica (2015).

the parish community seek a place, a corner where they can make a little apartment or, if there is no other option, rent a modest apartment for this family." These families, he said, "should be provided with a roof, welcomed and integrated into the community." He set an example by housing two refugee families at the Vatican, and, in his words, they will stay "until the Lord wants."[34]

Addressing priests and religious in Bosnia and Herzegovina, Pope Francis said:

> "The priest, the consecrated person, is called to live the anguish and the hope of the people; to work in concrete circumstances often characterized by tensions, discord, suspicions, insecurities and poverty. Faced with these painful situations, we ask God to grant us hearts that can be moved, capable of showing empathy; there is no greater witness than to be close to the spiritual and material needs of the faithful. It is the task of us bishops, priests and religious to make the people feel the nearness of God; to feel his comforting and healing hand; to be familiar with the wounds and tears of our people; to never tire of opening our hearts and offering a hand to all who ask us for help, and to all those who, perhaps because they feel ashamed, do not ask our help, but who are in great need of it."[35]

Nigerian bishops and clergy in particular need to do some critical reflection in this regard. Public scrutiny reminds the flag bearers of the Church that little has been done to make the poor Church really a Church for the poor. The recent outright removal from office of a diocesan bishop in Germany for his extravagant lifestyle and waste of Church funds sent signals across Christendom. Criticism helps us to be more authentic and execute change. Consequently, the car or house of the bishop or priest should not be the central symbols of the Church. Having and maintaining two (in some cases three) cars could be a demonstration of prosperity. Has it any connection with the many robberies of rectories and kidnapping of priests? For obvious reasons, "off-shore" apostolate is becoming more attractive, and sometimes it takes precedence over regular duties. The motives for the many Catholic prayer ministries nowadays are no longer discernible and transparent. Some are copying the prosperity churches in the name of conformism and opportunism. Those being copied emphasise that it is God's will and ordinance that all are destined to command wealth; being Christian today, it appears,

---

34 Accessed from: http://www.zenit.org/.
35 cf. Thomas Rosica (2015).

factors out self-denial, experience of want, suffering and cross. The affluence and bourgeoisie lifestyle of these ministers escape public scrutiny, so much so that the most gullible, the very poor and unenlightened sometimes give all they have (or even borrow) to pay tithe and/or "sow seeds." When t-shirts, scarves or almanacs are arbitrarily declared sacramentals, the abuses prior to the 16th century Reformation come to mind.

To be influenced by or succumb to what is in vogue ("Zeitgeist") is tantamount to lack of quintessence and orientation. History bears witness that whenever the Church lost focus, it paid heavily for it. It is now fashionable to do billboards and make expensive brochures during episcopal visits. The "killing of cows" *(igbu efi)* during *Cathedraticum*, as it is now, raises a number of questions. The burden of levies, parochial or diocesan, is becoming excruciating for many Catholics. In some cases and places, however, rich donors contribute hugely towards the erection of churches, rectories, halls, schools, and buying cars for newly ordained priests, etc. Some even finance them singlehandedly without strings attached, and this is commendable. Some financially buoyant parishes contemplate knocking down already dedicated churches and other structures in order to erect better ones. Since some parishes and communities have no modest place of worship or the like, solidarity demands that rich parishes partner with poorer ones. Some Europeans, especially those who are familiar with our material comfort and display of privileged circumstances, argue that our vocation boom is more a result of the societal prestige and economic benefits than one of self-sacrifice and religious vows.

Effective and credible priestly ministry manifests itself in radical simplicity and poverty. "Teachers of the faith need to get out of their cave," and the clergy "out of the sacristy." Authentic pastors should have the "odor of the sheep" if they are to be effective and credible. Pope Francis has ushered in a new urgency, passion, and authenticity to our mission today. For him, authentic power is service: "Power in the Church is not about who kisses one's hand but how many feet one can wash in the service of Christ."[36]

It is true and laudable that dioceses, parishes, and religious congregations are planning for the future by building up their financial base and

---

36 cf. Thomas Rosica (2015).

becoming less dependent on foreign aid. They do so by way of collections, launchings and fundraising events, levies, apartment blocks, real estate, stocks, banks, petrol stations, farming, gastronomy, etc. Without competent and transparent management, such investments can collapse and led to bankruptcy. Again, overly concentrating on financial self-independence can also distract from the actual mission of the Church. When the Church is no longer perceived as a community of believers, when bishops and priests cease to be spiritual leaders, then the sheep turn to alternative sources to quench their spiritual thirst.

4.4 Empowerment through Education and Participation

Empowerment has been described as "a desired process by which individuals, typically including the 'poorest of the poor', are to take direct control over their lives. Once 'empowered' to do so, poor people will then (hopefully) be able to be the agents of their own development."[37] It means enabling people to take direct action to meet their own needs. But such a successful process of empowerment must also involve changes in power structures at all levels: local, national, and international. Empowerment has to do with redistribution of power and transformation of institutions.

Gaudium et spes appeals to lay people to assume greater roles in the Church and in the world through "illuminating" initiatives (cf. GS 43). Bishops should mobilise the Knights and Ladies Auxiliary and such top-class members of the Church; within their rank and file are military personnel, police officers, politicians, business people, chiefs, etc. They can use their privileged positions to communicate the message of the Church, and in this way facilitate the Church's dialogue with government. Christians should be enabled to assume responsibility for their faith, and to take direct control over their lives through participatory village development interventions. Further than that, the Church, insists Bernard Munono,[38] should be courageous enough to seek dialogue with those responsible for injustices, denunciate their conduct both verbally and through pastoral letters, and

---

37 cf. Alan Thomas (2000).
38 Bernard Munono, ed., The Challenge of Justice and Peace: The Response of the Church in Africa Today, Published by the Pontifical Council for Justice and Peace, Vatican City, 1998.

organise peaceful demonstrations. Simultaneously, it has to educate the people about their basic human rights, inform government officials of their responsibilities, and develop structures to help people fight against abuse of their rights. Church leaders, human rights experts, journalists, writers, and broadcasters – all must proclaim the single, clear message: ordinary people must be empowered; ordinary people must be allowed to take control of their own lives. Only in this way can liberation from the sin of humanity opposed to solidarity take place. Proclaiming this message can be done through public discussions and seminars.

Formal education has been a key activity of the Church in countless primary, secondary and tertiary institutions. Just like health institutions run by the Church have contributed significantly to the development of the people, so also have Church-sponsored schools played and continue to play a dominant role in the educational sector; they are not involved in incessant strikes that have been the hallmark of our educational setup. Education that involves the acquisition of knowledge skills, attitudes and values, remains a key factor in development. The type of education a community offers to its members determines to a large extent, the rate, nature and direction of its development. This development education approach aims at raising the awareness of people in villages and urban compounds in order to help them identify their issues, plan together for projects, and cooperate in the implementation of plans. It is being sponsored by dioceses and Church groups. This approach should be intensified. Many poverty-stricken parents have no money to pay for the school fees of their children, and countless number of orphans are out of school and exposed to violence and exploitation. The children of the poor have a high probability of getting poorer as a result of the lack of access to good education, which limits them to substandard jobs. Financially buoyant parishes and institutions might think of organising scholarship schemes for such indigent children.

As agents of development, our dioceses should endeavour to continue their efforts of providing integral, ethical, and qualitative education to our future generation through new nursery/primary and post primary schools. This is because young people are a country's greatest wealth and their integral education is a fundamental necessity. Eradicating illiteracy, said Pope Benedict XVI, is one "particularly important way to combat the desperation that can take root in the hearts of young people, and that lies at the base of many individual or collective acts of violence."[39] Through its various educational institutions, the Catholic Church should be on the frontline, alongside men and women of good will, in the field of the integral formation of the young. Adequate steps should be taken to ensure that our children in public schools enjoy their rights of receiving Catholic education. The current focuses on adult and mass literacy by government, international governmental and non-governmental organisations should be encouraged. The Church may consider the establishment of skill acquisition centres as a way of contributing towards national manpower development and enhancing self-reliance among the unemployed.[40] However, merely technical and academic training is not enough, it is also important to promote education based on human and moral values.

The importance of the means of social communication in this education process cannot be overemphasised. They have a great potential for influencing public opinion. The mass media are influential and attractive to the young and most sections of society. According to the Second Vatican Council, teaching at all levels has benefited by their use and they contribute in "eliminating illiteracy and in providing both basic and further education." In developing countries like Nigeria, they help people "to achieve progress and freedom." The Council document further stresses that it is man's basic right to be informed and to seek information that is "full, consistent, accurate and true." With full knowledge of his situation and events, he is able to take right decisions and adapt himself to the real situation: "Only in this way can he assume a responsible and active role in his community and be a part of its economic, political, cultural and religious life."[41] The ethical principles and norms (solidarity, subsidiarity, justice, equality and responsibility) that govern other areas of life also govern the social means of communication. Care should be taken to see that these means of communication are not used to discriminate one group against another even though the needs and interests of one could be borne in mind.

While underlining the positive aspects and benefits of the internet, its risks such as rabble-rousing, mobbing, pornography, pedophilia, and

---

39 Accessed from: http://www.zenit.org/.
40 cf. Lucius I. Ugorji (2000).
41 *Inter mirifica*, Nr. 19.

violence should not be underestimated. Necessary steps, like filters, should be taken to protect minors. In the western world, family ties and traditional values are experiencing negative trends as a result of social networking and surfing on the internet. In the United Kingdom, teenagers and young people aged between 16 and 24 spend more than 27 hours a week on the internet.[42] Fuelled by an increasing use of tablets and smart phones, the number of Nigerians exposed to these social networks is rapidly increasing. Activities such as watching video clips online, playing games, instant messaging (via Twitter, WhatsApp, LinkedIn, Instagram or Tumblr and Facebook) and social media have driven growth in mobile internet use in the country. "Texting" via these media is influencing young people also negatively; for example, often in their formal writings, they make incomplete sentences, swap capital and small letters, spell words incorrectly, etc. Children and young people should not be left alone on these digital streets. There is a need for family pastoral ministries, teachers and parents to work together in dealing with the inherent dangers and problems. Most notably, priests, catechetical instructors, youth leaders and teachers can educate children and young people on the right use of these gadgets. Pulpits, Sunday evening instructions, classrooms and lecture halls as well as radio and TV media provide opportunities for such an education.

Church documents, encyclicals and general catechesis could also be communicated better through these means. Nevertheless, it is not enough to use these means of communication only for the spread of the Christian message and teachings of the Church. It is also important and necessary to integrate this message into those means. Most importantly, the Church in Nigeria should use traditional means of communication and languages in evangelisation. Although the Catholic press is still in its infancy in Nigeria, it is a primary vehicle of evangelisation in which no amount of investment is too much. Among other advantages, the Church would be able to project an image of mass media that is not infested by unethical and biased practices. In comparison to religious literature from outside which are beyond the reach of most, what is printed or re-printed within the country is usually within reach, hence the need for Catholic printing presses and publishing houses.

---

42 Accessed from: http://www.telegraph.co.uk/.

Fides (Awka diocese) now prints and circulates papal encyclicals. Bravo! Radio *sapientia* (Onitsha archdiocese) is already broadcasting. Congratulations! This medium and such still to come should embark on more than just airing Masses, Rosaries, and Angelus. Buying airtime both in Radio and TV for debates and discussions on burning issues that touch the lives of the people and using the documents and social teachings of the Church as solid materials and fundamentals is an invaluable means of evangelization. Establishing a TV network like "EWTN" (Eternal Word Television Network) with modern technology and professional management on the national or provincial level should be on the agenda of our bishops.

Empowerment and participation are closely linked. Participation is the "voluntary and generous engagement of a person in social interchange."[43] This participation in public life has a theological basis that lies in the fact that, as yeast, the Christian is called "to transform the world, with gospel of love, forgiveness, honesty, justice, respect for the dignity and right of the human person, integrity, faithfulness, trust in God, etc."[44] Participation is achieved through assuming personal responsibility in one's area of concern and taking an active part in public life. It is extremely important that the people be given every chance to exercise the initiative in identifying their basic problems and areas of need as a people of God in Nigeria. The identification and description of the problems should not be confused with the eventual prescription of their remedies. An active participation presupposes, above all, education and adherence to sound cultural values. Above all, participation plays a very central role in the eradication of poverty.[45]

4.5 Dialogue

Dialogue and cooperation between religions is very central to peace and justice in the world. Vatican II Council document *Nostra aetate* provided for the Catholic Church the theological basic principle. In a very special

---

43 *Catechism of the Catholic Church*, Nr. 1913.
44 cf. Lucius I. Ugorji (2000).
45 cf. Martin Joe Ibeh, Von der wirtschaftlichen Entwicklungshilfe zur umfassenden sozio-kulturellen Entwicklungspolitik – Ein Plädoyer, in: Martin Joe Ibeh/Joachim Wiemeyer (Hrsg.), Entwicklungszusammenarbeit im Zeitalter der Globalisierung, Schöningh Verlag Paderborn, 2006.

way, Pope John Paul II promoted interreligious dialogue. During his many trips to almost all African countries interreligious dialogue was a permanent agenda. The epoch-making gathering at Assisi (Italy) in September 1986 of leaders of five major religions – Buddhism, Christianity, Hinduism, Islam, and Judaism – and their joint declaration on Nature remain an eloquent example of an inter-religious action worthy of continuing at all levels. The Council and the first African Synod of 1991 have encouraged Congregations and Conferences of bishops to establish departments of ecumenism and interreligious dialogue at their secretariats. How effective they are is another question. The main objective is the establishment and maintenance of contacts between religious bodies and the empowerment of Church personnel and communities for genuine dialogue.

For the Catholic Church in Nigeria, the constant Communiqué after meetings are good but we need to change strategy. Its concern for social mission should go beyond hesitant official comments on burning issues. The Church's particular concern should be to defend the universal rights to life and to religious freedom, to freedom of speech and criticism, even within the Church. It should invest more on social justice, promote cooperatives and genuine private initiatives, empower interest groups and movements, read the signs of the times, monitor keenly developments in the market economy and prophetically denounce economic injustice and human degradation.

However, the social malaise that plagues our country transcends religious and ethnic boundaries. Constructive dialogue and cooperation are necessary. The Church should intensify its commitment to initiatives aimed at promoting dialogue, respect and cooperation between different religious groups; this is of particular importance in view of the diverse ethnic and religious affiliation of our population. Unfortunately, radical churches are disinterested and unwilling to engage in dialogue; they prefer to defend their position as true believers and castigate the rest as agents of the devil. The more fundamentalists win influence and power, the more difficult it is to engage in interreligious cooperation in development and social justice. To establish mutual respect for and peaceful coexistence with other believers, the Church should teach and educate people about the need and value of dialogue through witnessing with other religions (Christian and non-Christian), especially Islam and African Traditional Religion. Interreligious and cultural dialogue on fundamental elements of our national ethos should be pursued.

It is worth mentioning that some pilot projects have been undertaken to enhance dialogue and reconciliation. One of them is the documentary film, "The Imam and the Pastor" and the "Christian-Muslim Interfaith Mediation Center" in Kaduna. At the New Year General Assembly of German Bishops' Conference held in March 2014 in Münster, Kardinal, John Onaiyekan reported there are other local initiatives beyond religious boundaries undertaken by young men and women that aim at fighting the polarization of the country.[46] On the national level, however, it has not been possible for a Nigerian interreligious commission to produce a communiqué or an action plan for peace. Through dialogue, some local controversies in Anambra State have been successfully resolved; for example, the chieftaincy crisis *"ichi ọzọ"* (Onitsha ecclesiastical province), traditional marriage ritual *"ọkụkọ onye-ụwa"* and the mourning practice by widows *"mma ekwu."* Conversely, some controversial traditional practices have proven intractable to resolve, like the chieftaincy ritual *"mma nka,"* and burial rituals *"ikpo-nye aja"* and *"afụ na afụrọ."* This failure has caused serious divisions and separatism in some local churches, and has even cost human lives in some communities. As a result, the Church has to intensify its dialogue with all the traditional institutions involved.

5. Conclusion

The world has changed politically, socially, and culturally since Vatican II. Think of the cold war, space exploration, genetic engineering and biotechnologies, cybernetics and robotics, the digital revolution of the internet and telecommunication, and mass media! Negative trends also abound: impoverishing effects of the globalisation of financial capitalism and economic imperialism, conflicts and wars, fanaticism and acts of terrorism (with collateral damage), arms trading and proliferation, refugees and migration, global warming and environmental degradation. Most of these developments and problems of today were not there as Vatican II was convoked. In the face of these later developments, can the Council still provide a dependable agenda, a new course for inculturating the gospel?

---

46 cf. Wolfgang Schonecke (2014).

Hans-Joachim Höhn[47] calls attention to the fact that Jubilee celebration is not just about looking back at what happened in time, but is more of an occasion and opportunity to think about what at this present time is called for and should be done. Celebrating Vatican II is not just about reading the documents, it is more about applying the practice and methods of Vatican II. To see the Church as being there only for the timeless and eternal realities is a half-truth. Its duty is to look into the existential and social challenges facing the world here and now, and challenges of future relevance. In doing so, attention should be focused on proclamation that is timely and inspired by the gospel and sources of faith. *Gaudium et spes* has provided the principles and working tools.

A great deal is being said and done by the Church in Nigeria on the subject of justice and peace. An important aspect of evangelisation is to promote humanity – to help persons, communities, and institutions become more human. The Nigerian Church has been involved in this through its work to alleviate poverty, ignorance, and disease. It has sought to promote human living conditions and an awareness of human dignity. But more needs to be done.

Bibliography

Alan Thomas, Poverty and the 'end of development', in: Tim Allen and Alan Thomas, eds., Poverty and Development into the 21st Century, Oxford University Press in association with The Open University, Oxford, 2000.

Arno Anzenbacher, Christliche Sozialethik: Einführung und Prinzipien, Schöningh Verlag Paderborn, 1998.

Barnabas C.Okolo, Social Teachings in *Gaudium et spes*: The Nigerian Connection, in: Obiora F. Ike, ed., Catholic Social Teachings En-Route in Africa, Snaap Press Ltd., Enugu, 1991.

Bernard Munono, ed., The Challenge of Justice and Peace: The Response of the Church in Africa Today, Published by the Pontifical Council for Justice and Peace, Vatican City, 1998.

Hans-Joachim Höhn: Zwiespältig und unbequem – Wie feiert man angemessen ein Konzil? in: Herder Korrespondenz Spezial, 2012.

---

47 Hans-Joachim Höhn: Zwiespältig und unbequem – Wie feiert man angemessen ein Konzil? in: Herder Korrespondenz Spezial, 2012.

Herder Korrespondenz Spezial, *Konzil im Konflikt, 50 Jahre Zweites Vatikanum,* Oktober 2012.

Lucius I. Ugorji, The Memoirs of a Shepherd on Social Problems and Theological Themes of the Day, Snaap Press Ltd., Enugu, 2000.

Martin Joe U. Ibeh, Environmental Ethics and Politics in the Developing Countries. A Case Study from Nigeria, Schöningh Verlag Paderborn, 2003.

Martin Joe Ibeh, Von der wirtschaftlichen Entwicklungshilfe zur umfassenden sozio-kulturellen Entwicklungspolitik – Ein Plädoyer, in: Martin Joe Ibeh/Joachim Wiemeyer (Hrsg.), Entwicklungszusammenarbeit im Zeitalter der Globalisierung, Schöningh Verlag Paderborn, 2006.

Michael Sievernich, *Erst die Ouvertüre. Das Zweite Vatikanum als Konzil der Weltkirche?* in: Herder Korrespondenz Spezial, *Konzil im Konflikt, 50 Jahre Zweites Vatikanum,* Oktober 2012.

Reinhard Marx & Helge Wulsdorf, Christliche Sozialethik: Konturen – Prinzipien – Handlungsfelder, AMATECA Lehrbücher zur katholischen Theologie, Band XXI, Bonifatius GmbH Verlag Paderborn, 2002.

Thomas Rosica, *"Gaudium et Spes at 50": A keynote address delivered to the Association of United States Catholic Priests in St. Louis, Missouri on June 30th,* 2015, in: http://www.zenit.org/.

Wolfgang Schonecke, "Hat Toleranz noch eine Chance? Bedrohungen des christlich-islamischen Dialogs in Afrika," in: Herder Korrespondenz, Heft 6, Juni 2014.

Church Documents

Pope Benedikt XVI, *Address of His Holiness at the Meeting with the Parish Priests and the Clergy of Rome, Thursday, 14 February 2013,* in: http://w2.vatican.va/content/benedict-xvi/en.html.

Pope Francis, Pope Francis, *Address to priests and religious during a one-day pastoral visit to Bosnia and Herzegovina on June 6, 2015,* in: http://www.zenit.org/.

Pope Paul VI, *Populorum progressio* 1967.

Catechism of the Catholic Church, Geoffrey Chapman, London, 1994.

Communiqué of Seminar organised by the Episcopal Commission for Justice, Development and Peace of the Catholic Bishops' Conference of Nigeria (CBCN), Jos, 1996.

Compendium of the social doctrine of the Church, 2004.

Inter mirifica 1963.

Gaudium et spes 1965.

Web-References

http://www.vatican.va/index.html.

http://www.telegraph.co.uk/.

http://www.un.org/en/index.shtml.

http://www.zenit.org/.

https://en.wikipedia.org/.

Hyacinth E. Ichoku

When Evening Comes: Thinking of Retirement of Priests in Nigeria

1. Introduction

There is an impending welfare crisis in the Church in Nigeria, unless urgent and strategic steps are taken to avert this crisis. By 2021 some dioceses in the South East Nigeria will be having in excess of 40 priests retire and this will rise steadily for many more years. The vocation boom that started in the 1970s, particularly in the South Eastern Nigeria, has served the Church well in its ministry. It is now time to think and plan strategically for the future and retirement of the first cohort of generations of priests and the subsequent generations. Many of that generation are now showing signs of exhaustion; drained and sapped of their former energy and vigour, bent low by the burden of years of hard work, it is now time to find shelter. Retirement beckons! Is the Church in our land prepared to care for these gallant soldiers who have helped the Church to be what it is today? Does the Church in our land have the material, social, psychological, and spiritual apparatus to ensure that these men are happily retired and that those who follow them will have a reasonable expectation of what awaits them in retirement? I once met one of our more popular and dedicated priests in an elderly residence. Seeing me in soutane, he started shedding tears. I, in turn, was forced to shed tears for him in his living condition. Is this the nature of retirement for diocesan priests?

2. Meaning of Retirement for a Priest

By the very nature of their ordination commitment, priests do not retire from their priesthood in the sense that they cease to be priests. No, they remain priests but cease from active ministry. This is unlike retirement from secular service, where the individual retires to pursue a different line of trade or profession. This is because the priesthood is essentially a character. Not a profession or a trade. Resignation from pastoral office, therefore, does not imply resignation from the priesthood. Priests remain active for their own wellbeing and for the spiritual wellbeing of the people of God even in retirement.

This sense of being active even in retirement often blurs the line between retired and non-retired priests, as retirement suggests complete withdrawal from one's occupation or position upon reaching a certain age. Retirement, as popularly understood, is associated with formal occupation and hierarchical organization or division of labour. The sense of retirement for a priest is further blurred in the African context where occupation is a fluid concept. Even in contemporary Africa, there are no strict division of labour as in the industrialised western countries. In a subsistent economy, as prevailing in many African societies, there is an attempt to spread risk among many sectors of the economy. A wine taper is also a farmer, and a blacksmith at the same time. A diviner or fortune-teller may also be a weaver and a farmer. This lack of a clear cut division in occupation implies that retirement is not encompassed by the African orientation to work. A person keeps working until he is no longer able to work either on account of ill-health or age. At this age, the children take on the responsibility of caring for their aged parents. This family arrangement whereby the children become the guarantee of basic provisions at old age eliminates the urgency of saving and planning for old age among Africans. The idea of formal retirement could, therefore, be said to have come with westernisation and the establishment of paid formal work in African societies. This lack of a clear cut idea about retirement in African work and ethics, coupled with the idea of permanent priestly commitment, makes it difficult for the African catholic priest himself, much less the ordinary lay faithful, to think about and plan for the eventual retirement of the priest from active pastoral engagement. The consequence is that dioceses do not make a provision for or plan for the retirement of priests. Priests work until they have become so old that they are no longer capable of pastoral function.

3. Changing Environment

The situation is changing fast. Globalisation and the changing structure of the family unit as known before now are creating more independent individuals that are less attached to their roots and parents. This is creating a growing consciousness among the working population in the formal sectors of the economy and a sense for a need to plan for retirement outside of possible care being provided by their children. People are now planning and saving for their retirement.

The introduction in Nigeria of the contributory pension has helped in no small measure to foster an increasing consciousness about retirement. In the past, workers in the formal sector saw the meagre pension and gratuity government will provide in the distant horizon. It was all government responsibility. However, the current contributory pension schemes make it mandatory for the employer and employee to contribute a certain percentage to the workers' retirement benefit.[1] The monthly deductions from a worker's salary raises the consciousness of planning for retirement among workers. In spite of this rising consciousness, a lot of people are still stuck in the old mentality of relying on their children to take care of their retirement needs. This is not helped by the dominance of subsistence living and informal work among the working population.

Unfortunately, the catholic priest who has committed himself to a life of celibacy, without children of his own, does not have a fall-back position on retirement as his civil counterparts who have children to support him in his old age. This is more worrisome given the current rate of disintegration of the family system. Priests are often distanced from their families economically and socially. The increasing disintegration of family ties makes it more difficult today than before for the priest to hope for retirement support from their immediate biological family. The priest must therefore rely almost entirely on the Church to which he has dedicated his life to as a minister. This in itself creates a challenge for the dioceses as the number of priests who are looking for retirement support keeps increasing. Coupled with this is that unlike most dioceses abroad where priests receive formal income, pay taxes, and save towards their retirement and expect social protection from the government, most priests in our dioceses do not have any formal income and do not expect any form of social protection provisions from

---

1   This percentage was previously 7.5% each by the employer and employee in the Contributory Pension Act of 2004. The 2014 version of the Act stipulates 10% of the workers monthly earning to be contributed each by the employer and the employee.

the government. Most spend the little stipend they receive on charity and end up having no savings.

4. At What Age Should Priests Retire?

If it is necessary for priests to formally retire from active ministry, it is also pertinent to discuss the appropriate age for priests to retire. The official canonical language is that when a priest reaches 75 years, he must tender a resignation letter. In other words, the bar beyond which a priest cannot proceed in official active service is 75 years. This seems to suggest that priests can actually voluntarily retire before this age. There is little or no literature on priests' retirement or conditions under which they retire which could guide argument. However, there is evidence that in many developed countries, a large proportion of priests retire before this age. For example, a document issued by Bishop Eugene J Gerber of the catholic diocese of Wichita (USA) in 1992 and amended in 2003, stated that taking cognizance of the "uniqueness of each priest's aging process may demand/suggest an earlier retirement age" (i.e. earlier than 75). Although the document states that no priest should be forced to retire at age 70, it nevertheless states that

> "A priest who has reached his seventieth (70th) birthday is eligible for retirement. If a priest intends to retire at age seventy (70) or anytime thereafter, he must meet with the Bishop to plan for retirement at least six months in advance."

There are, on the other hand, dioceses that are raising the retirement age to 75. For example, Paulson (2009) reported that the Archdiocese of Boston was insisting that priests have to wait until the age of 75 to retire due to shortage of priests in the archdiocese. It was reported that it had closed nearly 20% of its parishes in the preceding five years on account of this shortage of priests.

Given the faster aging process in Africa, there is a strong need to consider an earlier than 75-year retirement age for the African priest. The average retirement age for civil workers is 60 years, and in special cases 65. The current age structure of the Nigeria population shows that only about 3% reach beyond age 65.[2] Although it could be argued that priests enjoy

---

2   See Demographics of Nigeria http://www.123independenceday.com/nigeria/ demography.html.

special privileges in terms of living standards that may likely make them live, on average, longer than the general population, a 70 years old retirement threshold seems justified on a number of fronts. The intensity of work and environment of the ministry in Nigeria, and elsewhere in Africa, is far different from those of the developed countries, where life is much more organised and there are many more recreational facilities to support the ministry of a priest. In Europe, for example, the priest is saddled with the ministry and is not concerned with many other issues, because the government usually provides for most of its populations.

In our case, the priest is everything and almost every need of the individual parishioner and even non-parishioner is brought to him. For example, in developed countries, the government provides social welfare for the poor and the indigent, schooling and health services are guaranteed for every citizen. The priest then focuses on the immediate spiritual needs of his parishioners. However, in our case, the priest is saddled with both the spiritual and material needs of the parishioners. He has to substitute for those social services where government fails, and government fails in many respects. This puts a lot of burden on the priest. Furthermore, the physical terrain of the ministry is more demanding. The rough roads in flung out stations and the population per priest make the life of the priest in Nigeria more difficult. On account of this intensive demand on the priest in Nigeria, and less facilities available for self-maintenance, it is natural for him to wear out earlier than his counterpart in the developed countries. Furthermore, the priest in Nigeria does not have the same level of access to health care as his counterpart in developed countries. The same reasons that support the retirement of priests in developed countries at age 70 will also more than support the retirement of priests at age 70 in less developed countries.

5. Demographics Trends of Priests in South Eastern Nigeria

The last three and a half decades have witnessed tremendous growth in vocation to the catholic priesthood in different parts of Nigeria, particularly in South-Eastern Nigeria. The boom started in trickles in the late 1960's and by the mid-1970's it was like a bang. In 1974, 20 priests were ordained in one ordination event in the then Onitsha archdiocese comprising the current Onitsha archdiocese, Awka and Nnewi dioceses. By 1978, Awka was carved out of Onitsha archdiocese and the number of priests ordained each year dramatically increased in response to the pastoral demands. By the mid-1980's, each of these two dioceses in the present Anambra state was ordaining more than 15 priests in a year. The number has continued to soar with the creation of the Nnewi diocese in 2001. A similar development has taken place in Owerri ecclesiastical province which, according to official records, had a total of about 152 priests in 1980, but by 2012/2013 had 1157 priests. Onitsha ecclesiastical province, according to official records, had about 212 priests in 1980, while the number has now grown to 1626. Figure 1 shows the growth in individual dioceses within the two ecclesiastical provinces that make up the core of South Eastern Nigeria.

Figure 1: The growth of vocation in South Eastern Nigeria 1980 to 2013.

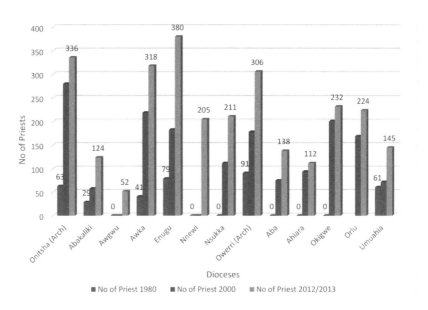

This figure shows that while Onitsha archdiocese had only 63 priests in 1980, this number grew to 366 in 2013. That is about a 533% increase between the two periods giving an average yearly increase of about 13 priests per year, or a compound growth rate of about 4.6% per year from 1980 to 2013. This is despite the fact that the Nnewi diocese was carved out of it by 2001. In other words, pulling the figures for Nnewi and Onitsha in 2013 would have resulted to a total of 860% increase in a space of 23 years.

Fig 2: Growth of Ordinations in the Awka Diocese between 1960 and 2010.

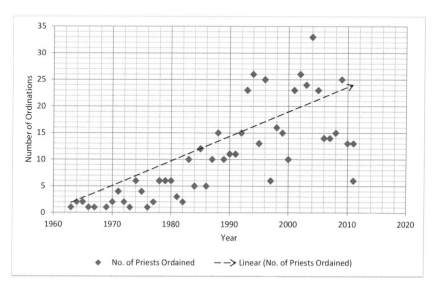

The growth in the number of ordinations in the Awka diocese is reflected in Figure 2, showing that there has been equally an outstanding growth in number of ordinations during the period. The dots in Figure 2 indicate the number of priests ordained in each year in the horizontal axis. The number of priests ordained is indicated in the vertical axis. The straight arrow line indicates the growth rate in number of priests during the period. The growth in the Owerri archdiocese has been less dramatic than the Onitsha archdiocese but is nevertheless very steep. The number of priests in the archdiocese grew from 91 in 1980 to about 306 in 2013. This is despite the split off of the Ahiara diocese in 1987. The Archdiocese increased by 336% during the period.

The growth rate in these dioceses is not about to ebb. If anything, it is likely to continue in an upward swing, given the growth rate of the general population of 2.8% which is one of the highest in the world, and also given the rate of unemployment among the educated youth, the prestige and social status that the catholic priesthood confers. The same rate of growth is also being experienced in other parts of Nigeria. The economic and social insecurities in the country tend to foster escalations in religious activities and choice of religious life and ministries generally in the society. In the Catholic Church, many dioceses, including those in northern Nigeria are today rejecting applicants for the seminaries due to a shortage of resources to keep and maintain the existing ministers.

The good side of this development is that, unlike Europe and other parts of the world where vocation to the catholic priesthood is waning, the Church in Nigeria is enjoying an unprecedented boom in vocations. There is increasing competition among villages and families to produce priests. The bishops are now increasingly finding it difficult to discern genuine vocation from pretenders because of the numbers putting themselves forward to be selected. The harvest is indeed rich and the labourers are also plenty!

In the face of this development, it is difficult to make a case for those who have laboured and are wearied, sapped and bent low from their many years of intensive work in the Lord's vineyard. This group of priests is increasing by day. The first generation of vocation boomers, those ordained in the mid-1970s, are now in their mid-sixties and late sixties and showing signs of tiredness. The first generation of priests, those ordained in the 1960's and early 1970's are already advanced in years. Many of them have reached their retirement age, but are confused and uncertain about whether they are regarded as retired, and what their fate will be in retirement.

Table 1: Projected No of Retired Priests in each Diocese by 2021 and 2031

Arch/Diocese	Year of Creation	No of Priest 1980	No of Priests 1990	No of Priest 2000	No of Priest 2012/2013	No of retired priests by 2021	No of retired priests by 2031
Onitsha (Arch)	1950	63	137	280	336	32	53
Abakaliki	1973	29	38	58	124	15	12
Awgwu	2005	0	0	0	52	0	0
Awka	1977	41	112	219	318	21	46
Enugu	1962	79	164	183	380	40	62
Nnewi	2001	0	0	0	205	0	0
Nsukka	1990	0	134	112	211	0	67
Owerri (Arch)	1950	91	75	178	306	46	15
Aba	1990	0	63	75	138	0	32

Arch/Diocese	Year of Creation	No of Priest 1980	No of Priests 1990	No of Priest 2000	No of Priest 2012/2013	No of retired priests by 2021	No of retired priests by 2031
Ahiara	1987	0	52	94	112	0	26
Okigwe	1981	0	94	201	232	0	47
Orlu	1980	0	95	169	224	0	48
Umuahia	1958	61	67	72	145	31	18
Total		364	1031	1641	2783	182	425

Table 1 computes estimates of the number of retired priests in each diocese by 2021 and 2031 based on retirement age of 70.

Given the foregoing argument for retirement at age 70, and assuming that priests are ordained at the average age of 29, the number of priests to retire by 2021 and 2031 in each of the dioceses in South-Eastern Nigeria has been computed in Table 1, columns 7 and 8. Column 7 is based on the number of priests in each diocese in 1980. A priest ordained in 1980 would have been born in 1951 at the latest. This places his retirement age in 2021. Note, however, that many of the priests were born earlier than 1951. Computing column 1 further assumes that the probability of survival of the cohort of priests ordained in 1980 or earlier is 0.5. That is, half of all the priests in this cohort will survive up to age 70. This group may be joined by a further group of priests who, though not reaching age 70, are too weak to continue active ministry on account of health challenges. This is a reasonable assumption, given that this is a special population group with a higher standard of living than the national average. Based on these premises, it is projected that the Onitsha archdiocese will have about 32 retired priests by 2021. The Awka diocese will have about 21 retired priests, and the Enugu diocese will have 40. In the Owerri province, the Owerri archdiocese will have 46 and the Umuahia will have 15. Some remnants of these retired priests will fall into the dioceses created out of the old ones. For example, we expect some older priests who opted to join the Nnewi diocese at its creation from Onitsha to have a few old priests who will retire by 2021.

Column 8 has been computed on the projection that about half of the priests ordained in or before 1980 who reach age 70 will survive up to age 80. This implies, for example, that of the 32 priests from the Onitsha archdiocese who survive up to age 70, half of them (16) will reach age 80 by 2031. In addition, about half of the 1990 cohort of priests will reach age 70 by 2031. This will bring the total number of retired priests in Onitsha by 2031 to 53. By the same calculation, Awka will have about 46 retired priests, Enugu will have 62, and Owerri will have less than expected (15), because the majority of its older priests joined Ahiara on its creation in 1987. The total number of retired priests in the two provinces, Onitsha and Owerri, will be about 425 by 2031. This is definitely a huge resource challenge, given the growing number of new priests being ordained each year, who also have to make resource demands on the dioceses to maintain them in the ministry.

6. Ecclesiastical Provisions[3]

The demographic trends among priests in South Eastern Nigeria described above make the need to plan for retirement of priests imperative. In the wider ecclesiastical context, the mission of the Church from its very beginnings has always included the care of the needy and the less privileged members of the society and among its own rank and file. Applied more narrowly, the obligation for provision for retirement of priests who have laboured in the service of the Church has become an emergent issue in the context of a potential explosion in the number of priests who are retired or are advancing fast towards retirement in our land. The rationale for these obligations is adumbrated in the various documents of the Church. Among other things, it helps the ministers themselves to develop a reasonable expectation of their future welfare and prospects, and are able to devote their lives more intensively for the ministry. According to Vatican Council II,

> "In countries where social security has not yet been adequately organized for the benefit of the Clergy, Episcopal Conferences are to make provisions for the setting up of diocesan organizations, the purpose of which is that under the supervision of the Hierarchy, satisfactory provision should be made for the proper support of Priests who suffer from sickness or old age… Priests should assist this organization when it has been set up, moved by the spirit of solidarity with their brother Priests, sharing their hardships…" (Presbyterorum Ordinis, No. 21).

---

3   This section relies on a similar article the author was invited to prepare on social protection for priests on retirement on the occasion of Msgr Aghazu's Diamond Jubilee celebration. An earlier version of it was presented to Awka Diocesan Presbyterium in 2013.

The Code of Canon Law similarly demands that "Suitable provisions are to be made for such social welfare as Priests may need in infirmity, sickness or old age" (Canon 281 par 1 CIC).

Conscious of this fundamental obligation, many dioceses around the world across developed and developing nations are increasingly seeking for ways to adequately cater to retired priests and priests who are health challenged. In a recent document from the archdiocese of Lingayen-Dagupan in the Philippines, the Archbishop observes that:

> "As an act of both equity and charity to Priests who have dedicated the best years of their lives to ecclesial service, Church Magisterium enjoins that as a sign of gratitude for their priestly labors and affirmation of their personal dedication, proper and decent financial support should be extended to them through a common fund specifically gathered and applied for this purpose according to need, during their retirement age, the more so when they become sick or disabled, until the Good Lord ultimately calls them to His Kingdom, in the spirit of the first Christian faithful in the pristine Church of Jerusalem where "they held everything in common" (Acts 4:32) and "distribution was made to each according to need" (Acts 4:35).

In a similar appeal from the diocese of Nottingham (UK), the bishop notes that:

> "Each diocese has a duty to look after its retired priests. In years gone by there were relatively more 'Mass goers' in relation to the number of priests to be supported and the "pay as you go" basis with the current year's collections paying for the current year's grants to the retired priests coped with the demand. We now have more retired priests in relation to those giving and this is expected to increase greatly in the next few years."

If dioceses in developed countries, that are far better resourced, are concerned about financing their retirement, how much more of need is there to plan in our case with our meagre resources? The demographic trends among priests and the religious in South East Nigeria require urgent attention to this impending welfare crisis that requires solid arrangements for the social protection of priests and the religious and the potential costs of fulfilling this important obligation.

7. The Challenge of Providing for Retirement

How do the dioceses intend to take care of the huge number of retired priests anticipated to occur in the next ten years? It will be difficult to imagine any other part of the world that will be facing more severe problems in this respect than the Church in South East Nigeria. The challenge is certainly beyond building structures for retired priests, often referred to as "Old Priests Home." This model of congregating retired priests in one place, as some dioceses are doing or planning to do, should be open to discussion. This model does not operate even in advanced countries with a long tradition of running retired people's homes, much less in our environment where the idea seems so foreign. Would diocesan priests who were not trained, *ab initio*, to live community life begin to learn that at old age? This model may be appropriate for religious congregations that have a long tradition of priests living in common. But will this be suitable for diocesan priests who are used to living alone or at most with one assistant or two in the parish? The adoption of this model in any diocese would seem to require extensive consultations particularly with prospective candidates who will use such facilities.

Experiences elsewhere in the region shows that many priests who are supposed to have retired are still clinging to their parishes. They want to retain control of parish resources because they are not sure of their welfare should they lose this power. Others who have braved retirement and relinquished their hold on parish resources or who have been forced to retire are living at the whims and caprices of younger priests who are "in charge." To put it straight, they live on charity and many who live this way are miserable. Many may be forced to depend on their relatives or friends for most of their basic needs. The truth is that our society is changing fast, and getting more westernised and individualistic. It is wishful thinking to leave the welfare of retired priests unplanned or to the charity of others.

The absence of any specific diocesan retirement plans for its priests may motivate some forward-looking young priests to become demotivated in the ministry. There might also be a tendency for younger generations of priests to resort to individual self-provision for their retirement. Such uncoordinated self-provisioning can result in unintended negative behaviour, and in fact, could undermine the gospel.

The main challenge of providing for retiring priests is financing their retirement. As the bishop of Nottingham notes, financing retirement of priests on a "pay as you go" basis is not sustainable. It is not a recharge card that one can buy at one time and not buy at another time. Sustainable financing means the ability to secure stable and sufficient financial resources and to allocate these resources in a timely manner to cover the cost of ensuring that retired priests are satisfied with their condition of material wellbeing.

Even where a diocese decides to congregate all the retired priests in one retirement home, funding it adequately will still create its own challenges. Apart from the requirements of feeding, medical, laundry, and other services, each priest will still need some pension scheme to provide his personal needs. There is also a skill gap in managing such a set up as few people are trained for managing such groups and old age institutions. Providing for the priests adequately requires a minimum regular income that could be paid to each individual priests on monthly, quarterly, or even weekly basis. The diocese alone cannot provide for all this. It requires that the priest himself must be involved in some kind of saving scheme to prepare for his retirement. This also demands on the priest to be forward-thinking. While the savings from these schemes may not be enough to provide for all that the priest needs, it will at least supplement the provisions by the diocese. There are various models of such saving schemes that a diocese might consider. The following briefly summarises the available schemes.

8. Models of Retirement Welfare Schemes for Priests

Possible retirement plans for a diocese to consider for its priests while in active service include: an Annuity Plan Scheme, a Deposit Administration Plan Scheme, and a Contributory Pension schemes.

8.1 Annuity Plans

An annuity is an insurance plan that pays out a steady stream of income to a subscriber on retirement in return for a series of payments in the form of investment made by the subscriber prior to retirement. Annuities are popular among investors who want to be sure that they continue to be assured some monthly, quarterly or biannual streams of income upon retirement.

To simplify matters, an annuity works this way: you make an investment in the form of an annuity plan with an insurance firm. It then makes payment to you in a future date or series of dates. Your annuity plan may specify that your income is paid to you monthly or quarterly or annually or that you receive it as a lump payment.

The amount of income you receive is determined by a number of factors including the length of your payment period. Some people choose to receive the payments for the rest of their lives, or for a defined number of years (e.g. 5, 10, 20 years). The amount you receive may also depend on whether you choose what is called a **fixed annuity**, in which case the amount of income you receive is a guaranteed payout. On the other hand, one may opt for a **variable annuity,** in which case you receive a variable sum depending on the yield on your initial investment which the firm invests on your behalf. In other words, under a variable annuity, you can receive a fluctuating series of income as your income will be tied to the performance of the overall market or group of investments.

There are two basic types of annuities: deferred annuity and immediate annuity. Under deferred annuity, your money is invested for a period of time before you can begin to make withdrawals from it, usually on retirement. Under an immediate annuity, you can begin to receive payments soon after you make your initial investment. This may happen, for example, for people who are already on the verge of retirement. Each of these basic types accommodates the fixed and variables payouts described above.

8.2 Deposit Administration Scheme (DAS)

The DAS is a long-term investment plan that ensures that workers have some income to fall back on when they retire. The accumulated investment enables the insured employee who has served for a minimum number of years from the commencement of the scheme to draw up to 50% of his/her contribution to meet urgent obligations; such as, healthcare service charges or school fees and other short-term commitments.

The DAS plan is usually available for employees within the 18–59 age range. The administration of the scheme is done in collaboration with the interested organisation. Some of the firms arrange to deduct premiums at the source. Since the deductions are made in proportion to the monthly salary of the employee, contributions made by employees automatically increase with an increase in salary.

If the employee's appointment is terminated or he/she chooses to retire, then in accordance with the scheme rules, he/she can choose to take either of the following benefits:

- Gratuity Benefit: This is a lump sum of money payable outright at the end of an employee's service.
- Annuity Benefit: This is a monthly income payable over a period of time (e.g. 5 or 10 years). The employee may also determine payments for a longer duration or even for life.
- Hybrid Benefit: This is a combination of 50% of the principal sum payable as a gratuity or an end-of-service benefit and the remaining part payable as an annuity benefit over a period determined by the employee.

An individual or a group may take out these insurance plans. In this case, the diocese may opt to cover every priest in the diocese with an underwriter (an insurance firm). It will also decide on how much to contribute as a premium per priest and for how long. It will also determine how long after retirement that each priest is to be paid a stream of income after retirement.

8.3 Contributory Pension Scheme

A very viable option for a diocese in Nigeria to consider is joining the National Pension Scheme. This is a scheme that covers federal and some state civil servants. The National Pension Act of 2004 established the contributory pension scheme for employees in the employment of the public and private sectors of the economy. The National Pension Act of 2004 has been amended as the Nation Pension Act of 2014. The Act stipulates that any employer with five or more employees should register with the National Pension Scheme. Specifically the Act stipulates that:

"Subject to Section 8 of this Act, the Scheme shall apply to all employees in the Public Service of the Federation, Federal Capital Territory and the Private Sector" and that "in the case of the Public Sector, who are in employment; and (h) in the case of the Private Sector, who are in employment in an organization in which there are 5 or more employees."

Thus, a diocese or a religious congregation as a private employer of labour may decide to join the National Pension Scheme through some of the Pension Administrators. However, being a contributory pension scheme, the Act stipulates that the employee contributes 7.5% while the employer contributes 7.5% of the monthly salary of the employee to the pension scheme. The employer may, however, decide to foot the entire bill for the scheme on behalf of the employee. In that case, the employer must remit

15% of the monthly salary of the employee to the Pension Fund. The amended version of the Act has, however, raised the percentage contributions by the employer and employee to 10% each. While it is recognised that priests do not earn a formal income, arrangements could be worked out with any of the Pension Administrators or Pension Managers to cover priests in a way that ensures that each priest saves some money towards retirement and benefits from these national retirement provisions. There is a need to investigate further the potential ways the individual priests and dioceses could benefit from the National Pension provisions.

8.4 Diocesan Pension Schemes

The Annuity and the DAS Plans and the National Contributory Pension Scheme provide feasible alternative platforms to ensure that priests and the religious who have spent their lives in the service of the gospel retire happily. Both the Annuity and DAS Plans involve taking out formal insurance coverage. The National Pension Scheme provides an attractive option because it removes the burden of managing the details and logistics of the scheme from the diocese, places it on experts in a big institution that will ensure that each priest receives a regular stream of income on retirement.

9. Diocesan Pension Foundation/Fund

In addition, a diocese might want to have the funding of its retired priests completely under its own control by floating a foundation that raises and manages funds for the retired priests. This requires a high level of technical skill in fund management, and not many dioceses have this level of skill. It requires a highly trained financial expert that is able to raise and invest funds in various portfolios to ensure that they yield maximum benefits to the foundation.

This is the model that is operated in many dioceses in developed and developing countries. In some of these dioceses, a common fund, Priests Retirement Foundation or Priests Retirement Fund is established under the diocesan management to provide retired priests financial support and to extend to them additional financial assistance when they are sick. This fund is dedicated entirely for this purpose and not mixed up with other diocesan funds. This operates as a solidarity foundation that depends entirely on the contributions made from various Church sources for this purpose. The funds raised are invested in interest yielding investments.

The foundation or fund specifies the amount of money to be paid out to each retired priest either on monthly, quarterly, or annual basis. In addition, they may be entitled to fees collected from some functions they perform and to some other forms of supplies. The Foundation also takes care of the Home of Aged Priests for those who wish to stay there. The rent for those who choose to retire in private apartments may be subsidised. In many instances where this kind of foundation operates, it is usually in addition to the usual old age pension and other benefits granted by the state. Unfortunately, there is no such social welfare provision in Nigeria for people who have not worked within the public sector of the economy.

9.1 Sources of Funds for the Foundation

The sources of funds for the Foundation is suggested to include:

- Monthly contributions from the parishes and chaplains in the diocese
- Monthly contributions of diocesan schools
- Contributions from the diocesan chancery
- Goodwill donations raised during fund raising campaigns
- Bequests from other priests and lay people

The fund is managed by a Board set up by the diocese and may be composed of the bishop of the diocese, the diocesan chancellor, two appointed priests and two or three lay people that are versed in investment and fund management.

9.2 Functions of the Board[4]

The main function of the Board of the Pension Scheme or Foundation is to oversee the business of the foundation in order to achieve its specified objectives. The specific functions include:

- To determine how much each parish pays into the fund.
- To collect and secure the contributions to the Foundation

---

4   Cf On Ald Priests' Retirement Foundation, Archdiocese of Lingayen-Dagupan (Philippines).

- To ensure monthly contributions and bequests to the scheme
- To decide on qualifications and conditions of benefit from the scheme
- To decide the amount and pay out for the monthly or quarterly benefits to those qualified to benefit from the scheme
- To secure and invest the funds of the foundation
- To render an annual account to presbyterium of the dioceses and other stakeholders.

While it is tempting for most dioceses to consider setting up a Retirement Foundation, the major problem with this alternative is that, given the high rate of priests that are expected to retire, it requires the diocese to accumulate large enough funds to ensure for adequate retirement benefits for the retiring priests.

10. Conclusion

The demographics of priests in Nigeria, particularly the South East, raises a major concern about retirement provisions in our dioceses. The vocation boom that started in the 1970's is now about to exert its toll on the dioceses in terms of providing for the first cohorts of this boom. Many of these great men have laboured in the Lord's Vineyard and are on the verge of taking their exit from active ministry. The challenge is how to ensure that they and those who follow them look forward to happy retirement. Unfortunately, many dioceses do not yet seem to factor this into their diocesan budgets. This paper is an attempt to raise consciousness about this important obligation that the dioceses owe to the men who have laboured to build the Church. Urgent steps need to be taken to make provisions for the material, psychological, and spiritual needs of these men.

Planning for the retirement of these priests requires careful considerations of all the available options. The beneficiaries of the plans must be part of the planning process. Their opinions matter about when, where, and how they retire.

Furthermore, there is a need to build in retirement plans into the program of serving and active ministers. This is crucial so that concerns about their future do not lead to counterproductive behaviour that undermines the ministry itself. Priests must be made to have a retirement savings account to prepare for their retirement, in addition to whatever other arrangement the diocese has for each one. This will reduce uncertainties about the future. Planning for retirement helps the priests to develop reasonable expectation about their future welfare; it makes them more confident in devoting their energies to the ministry.

References

Archdiocese of Lingayen-Dagupan (Philippines) (nd) On Ald Priests' Retirement Foundation.

Diocese of Nottingham (nd) Retired Priests Appeal.

Diocese of Portsmouth (2014) Priests' Retirement Fund Guidelines.

Federal Republic of Nigeria (2004) Pension Reform Act 2004.

Federal Republic of Nigeria (2014) Pension Reform Act 2014.

Ichoku HE (2013) Strategic Plan for Retirement of Priests in Awka Diocese: A Proposal. Paper presented to Awka Diocesan Priests, April 2013.

Ladd KL, Mertuzzi TV, Cooper D (2006) Retirement Issues for Roman Catholic Priests: A Theoretical and Qualitative Investigation, Review of Religious Research, 48(1) 82–104.

Paulson M (2009) Priests must wait till age 75 to retire, The Boston Globe, May 26, 2009.

Authors' Profiles

Augustine C. O. Oburota (PhD) is a priest of the Archdiocese of Onitsha. He has worked in the parish, was formator at the Bigard Memorial Seminary Enugu, Rector at Pope John Paul II Major Seminary, Okpuno, Awka South, and later Spiritual Director at the Holy Family Youth Village, Amansea, Awka North. Between 1991 and 1998, he was at the Catholic University of Louvain, Belgium, where he obtained his Master's and Doctorate degrees in Philosophy, specializing in Ancient Greek Philosophy. He also holds an Advanced Diploma in Education, University of London. Currently, he is on sabbatical leave in Germany.

Chike John Akunyili is a Medical Doctor and Director of long standing experience and husband of the late Dora Akunyili. He obtained his MBBS from the University of Nigeria and worked in the University of Nigeria Teaching Hospital for a long time before he went into private practice. He is the founder and Chief Medical Director of the St Leo Hospital, Trans Ekulu, Enugu, Nigeria. He worked very closely with PD Akpunonu to establish the health facility for seminarians when PD was the Rector of Bigard Memorial Seminary Enugu. He uses his medical practice to assist the Church in several capacities and enjoys a good relationship with Church personnel.

Emmanue Dim was ordained a priest for Awka Diocese, Anambra State, Nigeria, in 1989 and is currently the Rector of Tansi Major Seminary Onitsha. He holds a B.Phil, and BD of Urban University Rome. After a brief teaching period in St. Dominic Savior Minor Seminary, Akpu, he worked as Parochial Vicar and later as the Parish priest of St. Mary's Catholic Church Ufuma. He was sent to study Biblical languages in CIWA during the 1994/95 academic session. He went on to obtain a Licenciate in Secred Scripture (LSS) from the Pontifical Biblical Institute, Rome in 1999. He also obtained a PhD from the Pontifical Gregorian University, Rome in 2004 with specialisation in Old Testament Studies. He was appointed to teach in Tansi Seminary in 2004 and became the Vice Rector of the Institution from 2007 to 2014 and was appointed Rector in 2014. He has published four monographs in addition to several journal publications.

Hyacinth Eme Ichoku is a priest of Awka Diocese and Professor of Economics at the University of Nigeria, Nsukka. In addition to B.Phil and BD from Urban University (Rome), he holds a B.Sc and a M.Sc. in Economics from the University of Nigeria, Nsukka. He obtained a M.Soc Sc in 2000 and a PhD in 2006 from the University of Cape Town (South Africa). He became a Professor in 2012 with a specialisation in Health Financing and Development Microeconomics. Prior to going to study economics in 1992, he worked in the Catholic Institute of West Africa (CIWA) as Bursar (1989–1992). He was the Acting Director of Academic Planning, University of Nigeria (2011–2014). He is currently the Director, University of Nigeria Institute of Maritime Studies. He serves as chairman or member of several University of Nigeria Committees. He has served as consultant to many local and international development organisations including the Federal Ministry of Health, the World Bank, World Health Organization (WHO), United States Agency for International Development (USAID), and Department for International Development (DFID). He has published extensively in highly rated international journals and presented papers at over 30 international conferences. He is a member of the Catholic Bishops' Conference of Nigeria Finance Council and Board of Salus Trust Ltd, a Health Management Organization providing health insurance in Nigeria.

Ignatius M. C. Obinwa is a priest of the Catholic Diocese of Nnewi, Nigeria. He obtained a doctorate degree (*Dr. Theol.*) in Old Testament Studies from the *Philosophisch-Theologische Hochschule Sankt Georgen*, Frankfurt, Germany in 2001. He returned home and was called to serve as the Rector of Blessed Iwene Tansi Major Seminary, Onitsha, Nigeria (2001–2007). He later went on study leave to the University of Augsburg, Germany where he successfully did the German professorial programme known as *Habilitation* (2007–2011), at the end of which he was given, in line with the German academic system, a second doctorate degree in Biblical Studies (*Dr. habil.*) and also the *Lehrbefugnis*, which is the *authorisation* to hold a professorial chair in Biblical Studies in any German University. But he chose to return home to Nigeria, and from 2012 to present, he has been lecturing in the Biblical Department of the Catholic Institute of West Africa (CIWA), Port Harcourt, Nigeria.

Luke Emehiele Ijezie (B.Phil.; B.D.; LSS; STD) is a priest of the Catholic Diocese of Orlu, Nigeria. He studied Sacred Scripture at the Pontifical Biblical Institute (Biblicum), Rome, and Oriental Languages in Rome and Jerusalem. He is a member of many reputable academic associations around the world, including Society of Biblical Literature (SBL), Catholic Biblical Association of America (CBA), Pan-African Association of Catholic Exegetes (PACE), Association of African Theologians (ATA), Catholic Biblical Association of Nigeria (CABAN), and Catholic Theological Association of Nigeria (CATHAN). He is the National Secretary of CABAN, Chief Editor of the Annual CATHAN Proceedings and editor and publisher of the theological Journal, BIRD. Ijezie is the author of over 40 publications, including articles and books, and is one of the regular Abstractors for *Old Testament Abstracts* (OTA), an international biblical periodical. He currently teaches Sacred Scripture and Biblical Languages at the Catholic Institute of West Africa (CIWA), Port Harcourt.

Martin Joe U. Ibeh, a priest of Awka Diocese, obtained his B.Phil and BD from Urban University, Rome. He got his PhD in Paderborn, Germany in 2002, specialising in Social Ethics. He researches socio-ethical issues and has authored many publications. Currently, he is a Parish Administrator in the Catholic Diocese of Trier, Germany. Since 2005, he is the Chairman of "Beginn e.V.," a Non-Governmental Organization (NGO) in Germany, which funds educational and scholarship schemes for children and young people as well as health projects in Anambra State and beyond.

Matthew Obiekezie, BD (Theology), MA (Theology), MSc (Sociology), STL (Theology), PD (Educational Administration), and Ed.D (Educational Administration). Fr. Matthew Obiekezie, holds a doctoral degree from St. John's University, New York. A native of Awkuzu in Oyi L.G.A., Nigeria, he was ordained priest in 1985 for the Archdiocese of Onitsha. He has worked as pastor and manager of schools in some parishes where he worked in the Archdiocese of Onitsha. He worked as the Head of the Bursary Department in the Catholic Institute of West Africa (CIWA), Port Harcourt from 1995–1997. During his work in CIWA, he completed a case study – *Ethnicity in CIWA Administration: A Sociological Investigation* – with the

University of Port Harcourt, Port Harcourt (1997). He is currently the pastor of St. Jude Church, Abube Agu, Nando.

Patrick C. Chibuko is a priest of the Catholic Diocese of Enugu, Nigeria. He trained for the priesthood at St. Joseph's Major Seminary, Ikot Ekpene and Bigard Memorial Seminary Enugu and became ordained on July 10, 1983. He obtained his Bachelor of Divinity (B.D) from the Pontifical Urban University, Rome in June, 1983. He studied and specialised in Sacred Liturgy and obtained his Licentiate in Sacred Liturgy (LSL) from Pontifical University of St. Anselm, Rome in May, 1989 and Doctorate Degree in Sacred Liturgy (DSL) from the same university in Dec 13, 1990. Later in May, 1991, he obtained Bachelor of Philosophy (B. Phil) from Pontifical Urban University Rome. He joined the Academic Staff of the Catholic Institute of West Africa (CIWA), Port Harcourt, Nigeria since 1991 until now. He became a Professor of Sacred Liturgy in April 21, 2012. Currently, he is the Academic Dean and Head of Department of Sacred Liturgy in CIWA. He has published about a dozen books, 20 monographs and over 50 articles in local and international journals. He is also the Chairman of Enugu Diocesan Liturgy Commission and the Enugu Diocesan Master of Liturgical Ceremonies.

Abbreviations

AECAWA	Association of Episcopal Conferences of Anglophone West Africa
ATA	Association of African Theologians
B.Phil.	Bachelor of Philosophy
BD	Bachelor of Divinity
B.Sc.	Bachelor of Science
CABAN	Catholic Biblical Association of Nigeria
CATHAN	Catholic Theological Association of Nigeria
CBA	Catholic Biblical Association of America
CBCN	Catholic Bishops Conference of Nigeria
CIWA	Catholic Institute of West Africa
CMO	Catholic Men Organization
CWO	Catholic Women Organization
CSSp	Congregation of the Holy Ghost
CUWA	Catholic University of West Africa
DFID	Department for International Development
DSL	Doctorate Degree in Sacred Liturgy
Dr.	Doctor
Ed.D	Doctor of Education
Fr.	Father
G.M.	Gold Medalist
LSL	Licentiate in Sacred Liturgy
LSS	Licentiate of Sacred Scripture
MA	Master of Arts
MBBS	Bachelor of Medicine, Bachelor of Surgery
M.Sc.	Master of Science
M.Soc. Sc	Master of Social Science
missio	German branch of the Pontifical Mission Societies
Msgr.	Monsignor
NGO	Non-Governmental Organization
NT	New Testament
OT	Old Testament

OTA	Old Testament Abstracts
PACE	Pan-African Association of Catholic Exegetes
PhD, Ph.D.	Doctor of Philosophy
Prof.	Professor
Rev. Fr.	Reverend Father
SBL	Society of Biblical Literature
SECAM	Symposium of Episcopal Conferences of Africa and Madagascar
STD	Doctor of Sacred Theology
STL	Licentiate of Sacred Theology
USAID	United States Agency for International Development
WHO	World Health Organization
YHWH	Yahweh